Copyright: Rawda Press 2018
ISBN: 978-0-9929736-5-0
UK RRP: £9.95

Published by:
Rawda Press
62 Church Road
London E12 6AF
0207 998 7768
info@alrawda.org

Title: **Prophetic Matrimony**
                - 40 Hadith on Marital Harmony -

Author: Moin Uddin Khan

ISBN: 978-0-9929736-5-0

Published by: Rawda Press *(Imprint of IDEA Press)*

Cover Design: *LionSon*

Printed by: Mega Printers, Turkey

PROPHETIC MATRIMONY

40 HADĪTH ON MARITAL HARMONY

TRANSLATION & NOTES BY
MOIN UDDIN KHAN

Dedicated to our wives…
May Allah make them the coolness of our eyes.

"Our Lord, grant us in our spouses
and our offspring coolness of our eyes,
and make us an example for the righteous."

Al-Qur'an s25 v74

CONTENTS

Author's Note

اَلسَّـــلَامُ عَلَيْكُمْ وَرَحْمَةُ اللهِ وَبَرَكَاتُهُ

All praise is due to Allah, Lord of the worlds, we praise him and seek his aid and we send salutations upon his beloved messenger Muhammad, the chosen one, peace and blessings of Allah be upon him and his family, companions and all those who follow them in guidance.

Marriage is a sacred union that safeguards society and ensures the preservation of humanity. Islam has encouraged marriage and has provided much guidance on the topic. While there are many works on marriage; I found that most of them cover the rituals, rites and legalities of marriage which is a necessity to implement the ceremony and contract. Yet there are little works in the English medium providing support after the hype and glitter fades and the spouses are faced with the reality of living together. People assume that after marriage the couple automatically fall in love with each other like a fairy tale, while the truth is that the marital relationship needs time, dedication, sacrifice, patience and mutual tolerance to secure itself, especially in the initial critical stages.

This compilation seeks to highlight how the prophet ﷺ behaved with expressions and gestures of kindness, love and intimacy. By acting upon these hadith, one can hope that not only will they achieve closeness to Allah by emulating His messenger ﷺ, but one can also build their bond with their spouses in this world and also be in each other's company in the hereafter.

Moin Uddin Khan
Shawwal 1439 / July 2018

الحديثُ الأولُ

حَدَّثَنَا الْحُمَيْدِيُّ عَبْدُ اللَّهِ بْنُ الزُّبَيْرِ، قَالَ: حَدَّثَنَا سُفْيَانُ، قَالَ: حَدَّثَنَا يَحْيَى بْنُ سَعِيدٍ الْأَنْصَارِيُّ، قَالَ: أَخْبَرَنِي مُحَمَّدُ بْنُ إِبْرَاهِيمَ التَّيْمِيُّ، أَنَّهُ سَمِعَ عَلْقَمَةَ بْنَ وَقَّاصٍ اللَّيْثِيَّ، يَقُولُ: سَمِعْتُ عُمَرَ بْنَ الْخَطَّابِ رَضِيَ اللَّهُ عَنْهُ عَلَى الْمِنْبَرِ قَالَ: سَمِعْتُ رَسُولَ اللَّهِ صَلَّى اللَّهُ عَلَيْهِ وَسَلَّمَ يَقُولُ: إِنَّمَا الْأَعْمَالُ بِالنِّيَّاتِ، وَإِنَّمَا لِكُلِّ امْرِئٍ مَا نَوَى، فَمَنْ كَانَتْ هِجْرَتُهُ إِلَى دُنْيَا يُصِيبُهَا، أَوْ إِلَى امْرَأَةٍ يَنْكِحُهَا، فَهِجْرَتُهُ إِلَى مَا هَاجَرَ إِلَيْهِ

~ Hadīth 1 ~

INTENTION

Narrated by `Umar bin Al-Khattab:
I heard the Messenger of Allah ﷺ say, "The reward
of deeds depends upon their intentions and every
person will get the reward according to what they have
intended. So whoever's migration was for a worldly
benefit or for a woman to marry, his migration was for
whatever he migrated for."

Sahih al-Bukhari 1

Notes: Allah created the spouse from themselves so that they
may seek comfort and harmony in each other, and He created
love and mercy between them:

وَمِنْ آيَاتِهِ أَنْ خَلَقَ لَكُم مِّنْ أَنفُسِكُمْ أَزْوَاجًا لِّتَسْكُنُوا إِلَيْهَا وَجَعَلَ بَيْنَكُم مَّوَدَّةً وَرَحْمَةً

*And of His signs is that He created for you from yourselves mates that
you may find tranquillity in them; and He placed between you affection
and mercy.* (Al-Quran s30 v21)

Marriage like any other form of worship requires the right
intention in order to gain the reward from Allah, but it also
needs the right intention for the bond to build and for the
marriage to flourish.

The intention of marriage should be to seek what Allah has
made *halal,* to follow the *sunnah* of the Prophet ﷺ, seeking to
safeguard one's chastity and to seek pious children. The Prophet
ﷺ advised against having the wrong intention;

لَا تَزَوَّجُوا النِّسَاءَ لِحُسْنِهِنَّ فَعَسَى حُسْنُهُنَّ أَنْ يُرْدِيَهُنَّ وَلَا تَزَوَّجُوهُنَّ لِأَمْوَالِهِنَّ فَعَسَى أَمْوَالُهُنَّ
أَنْ تُطْغِيَهُنَّ وَلَكِنْ تَزَوَّجُوهُنَّ عَلَى الدِّينِ

*"Do not marry women for their beauty for it may lead to their doom.
Do not marry them for their wealth, for it may lead them to fall into
sin. Rather, marry them for their religion".* (Sunan Ibn Majah 1859)

2

الحديث الثاني

حَدَّثَنَا أَحْمَدُ بْنُ الْأَزْهَرِ قَالَ: حَدَّثَنَا آدَمُ قَالَ: حَدَّثَنَا عِيسَى بْنُ مَيْمُونٍ، عَنِ الْقَاسِمِ، عَنْ عَائِشَةَ، قَالَتْ: قَالَ رَسُولُ اللَّهِ صَلَّى اللَّهُ عَلَيْهِ وَسَلَّمَ: النِّكَاحُ مِنْ سُنَّتِي، فَمَنْ لَمْ يَعْمَلْ بِسُنَّتِي فَلَيْسَ مِنِّي، وَتَزَوَّجُوا، فَإِنِّي مُكَاثِرٌ بِكُمُ الْأُمَمَ، وَمَنْ كَانَ ذَا طَوْلٍ فَلْيَنْكِحْ، وَمَنْ لَمْ يَجِدْ فَعَلَيْهِ بِالصِّيَامِ، فَإِنَّ الصَّوْمَ لَهُ وِجَاءٌ

~ *Hadīth 2* ~

FOLLOWING THE *SUNNAH*

Narrated by 'Aisha:
The Messenger of Allah ﷺ said: "Marriage is a part of my *sunnah*, and whoever does not follow my *sunnah* has nothing to do with me. Get married, for I will boast of your great numbers before the other nations. Whoever has the means, let him get married, and whoever does not, then they should observe fast for it will be a shield for them (control their desire.)"

Sunan Ibn Majah 1846

Notes: One's intention in marriage should be to follow the *sunnah* of the Prophet ﷺ in their married life and to implement these teachings wholeheartedly. Marriage is not only a *sunnah* of the Prophet Muhammad ﷺ, but it was the *sunnah* of all the messengers of Allah. Allah says in the Quran:

وَلَقَدْ أَرْسَلْنَا رُسُلاً مِنْ قَبْلِكَ وَجَعَلْنَا لَهُمْ أَزْوَاجًا وَذُرِّيَّةً

'And indeed We sent Messengers before you, and made for them wives and offspring.' (Al-Quran s13 v38)

Allah informs us that He will love those who follow the sunnah:

قُلْ إِن كُنتُمْ تُحِبُّونَ اللَّهَ فَاتَّبِعُونِي يُحْبِبْكُمُ اللَّهُ وَيَغْفِرْ لَكُمْ ذُنُوبَكُمْ ۗ وَاللَّهُ غَفُورٌ رَّحِيمٌ

Say, "If you love Allah, then follow me, so Allah will love you and forgive you your sins. And Allah is Forgiving and Merciful."
(Al-Quran s3 v31)

One who is financially capable to get married should hasten to do so. Rather, it is actually through marriage that the spouses receive blessings, as the Prophet ﷺ said:

تَزَوَّجُوا النِّسَاءَ فَإِنَّهُنَّ يَأْتِينَكُمْ بِالْمَالِ

"Get married, as wealth comes with a spouse"
(Mustadrak 'ala al-Sahihain 2679)

الحَدِيثُ الثَّالِثُ

حَدَّثَنَا عَبْدُ اللَّهِ بْنُ يُوسُفَ، حَدَّثَنَا اللَّيْثُ، قَالَ: حَدَّثَنِي يَزِيدُ بْنُ أَبِي حَبِيبٍ، عَنْ أَبِي الخَيْرِ، عَنْ عُقْبَةَ بْنِ عَامِرٍ رَضِيَ اللَّهُ عَنْهُ، قَالَ

قَالَ رَسُولُ اللَّهِ صَلَّى اللَّهُ عَلَيْهِ وَسَلَّمَ أَحَقُّ الشُّرُوطِ أَنْ تُوفُوا بِهِ مَا اسْتَحْلَلْتُمْ بِهِ الفُرُوجَ

~ *Hadīth 3* ~

COMMITMENT TO SPOUSE

Narrated by `Uqba bin 'Amir:
The Messenger of Allah ﷺ said, "The most worthy
commitment to be loyal to, is that which makes marital
relationship lawful. (i.e marriage contract)"

Sahih al-Bukhari 2721

Notes: Marriage is one of the most sacred commitments one can
make after the commitment one makes to Allah; that we do not
worship others besides Him.

وَاعْبُدُوا اللَّهَ وَلَا تُشْرِكُوا بِهِ شَيْئًا

"Worship Allah and associate nothing with Him." Al-Quran s4 v36)
Likewise the marital bond needs commitment as well as effort
and sacrifice. Spouses should aim to stay loyal to each other by
not betraying each others secrets and trust, not to give up on each
other and to stay at each others sides through thick and thin. This
commitment should not be taken lightly as Allah reminds us
about staying true to our commitments:

يَا أَيُّهَا الَّذِينَ آمَنُوا أَوْفُوا بِالْعُقُودِ

"O you who have believed, fulfil commitments." (Al-Qur'an s5 v1)
It is through overcoming our differences and difficulties in the
initial stages of marriage that the relationship begins to mature
and develop into a caring and harmonious relationship. Part
of the commitment is to bear with each other until one sees the
blessings.

الحديث الرابع

حَدَّثَنَا هِشَامُ بْنُ عَمَّارٍ قَالَ: حَدَّثَنَا صَدَقَةُ بْنُ خَالِدٍ قَالَ: حَدَّثَنَا عُثْمَانُ بْنُ أَبِي الْعَاتِكَةِ، عَنْ عَلِيِّ بْنِ يَزِيدَ، عَنِ الْقَاسِمِ، عَنْ أَبِي أُمَامَةَ، عَنِ النَّبِيِّ صَلَّى اللهُ عَلَيْهِ وَسَلَّمَ أَنَّهُ كَانَ يَقُولُ

مَا اسْتَفَادَ الْمُؤْمِنُ بَعْدَ تَقْوَى اللَّهِ خَيْرًا لَهُ مِنْ زَوْجَةٍ صَالِحَةٍ، إِنْ أَمَرَهَا أَطَاعَتْهُ، وَإِنْ نَظَرَ إِلَيْهَا سَرَّتْهُ، وَإِنْ أَقْسَمَ عَلَيْهَا أَبَرَّتْهُ، وَإِنْ غَابَ عَنْهَا نَصَحَتْهُ فِي نَفْسِهَا وَمَالِهِ

~ Hadīth 4 ~

LOYALTY TO SPOUSE

Narrated by Abu Umamah:
The Prophet ﷺ would say, "Nothing is more beneficial to a believer after Taqwa of Allah, than to have a righteous wife who obeys him when he asks, who pleases him when he looks at her, who fulfils the oath he makes regarding her, and who is loyal to him with herself and his wealth in his absence."

Sunan Ibn Majah 1857

Notes: Islam encourages keeping ties of kinship with relatives and cousins, and that there is nothing wrong with having friends whose company one enjoys. However one must also commit time and effort into building the marital relationship. This can initially be difficult as the spouses may not fully understand each other, and therefore not be able to appreciate each other's company, which can lead to preferring others over one's spouse and creating a distance between them.

The Prophet ﷺ mentions in another hadith:

مَنْ يَضْمَنْ لِي مَا بَيْنَ لَحْيَيْهِ وَمَا بَيْنَ رِجْلَيْهِ أَضْمَنْ لَهُ الْجَنَّةَ

"Whoever can guarantee the chastity of their tongue and their private parts; I guarantee them paradise." (Sahih al-Bukhari 6474)

The husband and wife should maintain loyalty to their commitment in the sight of Allah, they should give each other the love and care this commitment demands and that they should not betray each other by giving this loyalty to anyone else. Thus other family and friends might not like one's spouse due to whatever reasons, in such situations one has to show their loyalty to their spouse as marital relationship needs to be prioritised with trust, benefit of doubt and positive thoughts about each other.

الحديث الخامس

حَدَّثَنِي مُحَمَّدُ بْنُ عَبْدِ اللّٰهِ بْنِ نُمَيْرٍ الْهَمْدَانِيُّ، حَدَّثَنَا عَبْدُ اللّٰهِ بْنُ يَزِيدَ، حَدَّثَنَا حَيْوَةُ، أَخْبَرَنِي شُرَحْبِيلُ بْنُ شَرِيكٍ، أَنَّهُ سَمِعَ أَبَا عَبْدِ الرَّحْمٰنِ الْحُبُلِيَّ، يُحَدِّثُ عَنْ عَبْدِ اللّٰهِ بْنِ عَمْرٍو، أَنَّ رَسُولَ اللّٰهِ صَلَّى اللّٰهُ عَلَيْهِ وَسَلَّمَ، قَالَ

الدُّنْيَا مَتَاعٌ، وَخَيْرُ مَتَاعِ الدُّنْيَا الْمَرْأَةُ الصَّالِحَةُ

~ Hadīth 5 ~

SPOUSE IS THE BEST PROVISION

Narrated by 'Abdullah bin 'Amr bin Al-' As:
The Messenger of Allah ﷺ said: "This world is a
provision, and the best of its provision is a righteous
woman."

Sahih Muslim 1467

Notes: Having a righteous spouse is a blessing and makes a
significant impact on oneself through positive influence, helps
towards the Islamic *tarbiya* of one's children, and develop a
harmonious Islamic environment in the home.

This *hadith* shows the lofty status and the respect Islam gives
to women as their role as a wife. Women not only lay the
foundation of the Muslim household but also via the role of a
wife and a mother, they impact society and the future generations
to come. The Prophet ﷺ stated this:

مَنْ رَزَقَهُ اللَّهُ امْرَأَةً صَالِحَةً، فَقَدْ أَعَانَهُ عَلَى شَطْرِ دِينِهِ، فَلْيَتَّقِ اللَّهَ فِي الشَّطْرِ الثَّانِي

*"Whomever Allah has blessed with a righteous wife, He has helped him
with half of his religion, so let him fear Allah with regard to the other
half."*(Al Mustadrak 'ala al-Sahihain 2681)

Choosing righteousness can help the spouses lead a respectful,
fruitful and a harmonious life as their expectations of greater
reward lies in the hereafter with their Lord. On the other hand
beauty, wealth and position will perish with time and the thing
that was sought will no longer be there, thus no satisfaction will
be gained.

الحديث السادس

حَدَّثَنَا أَبُو بِشْرٍ بَكْرُ بْنُ خَلَفٍ وَمُحَمَّدُ بْنُ يَحْيَى، قَالَا: حَدَّثَنَا أَبُو عَاصِمٍ، عَنْ جَعْفَرِ بْنِ يَحْيَى بْنِ ثَوْبَانَ، عَنْ عَمِّهِ عُمَارَةَ بْنِ ثَوْبَانَ، عَنْ عَطَاءٍ، عَنِ ابْنِ عَبَّاسٍ، عَنِ النَّبِيِّ صَلَّى اللهُ عَلَيْهِ وَسَلَّمَ، قَالَ: خَيْرُكُمْ خَيْرُكُمْ لِأَهْلِهِ، وَأَنَا خَيْرُكُمْ لِأَهْلِي

~ *Hadīth 6* ~

GOOD TO ONE'S SPOUSE

Narrated by Ibn 'Abbas:
The Prophet ﷺ said: "The best of you is the one who is
best to his wife, and I am good to my wives."

Sunan Ibn Majah 1977

Notes: Allah has sent Prophet Muhammad ﷺ as a role model
and an example for all of mankind. Allah says;

لَقَدْ كَانَ لَكُمْ فِي رَسُولِ اللَّهِ أُسْوَةٌ حَسَنَةٌ لِّمَن كَانَ يَرْجُو اللَّهَ وَالْيَوْمَ الْآخِرَ وَذَكَرَ اللَّهَ كَثِيرًا

*"There has certainly been for you in the Messenger of Allah an excellent
example for anyone who has hope in Allah and the Last Day and
remembers Allah often."* (Al-Qur'an s33 v21)

One needs to look at his practice as mentioned previously, the
Prophet ﷺ never struck his wives nor was he bad to them. Rather
he ﷺ mentions how women are made to be beloved to him:

حُبِّبَ إِلَيَّ النِّسَاءُ وَالطِّيبُ

"Women and perfume have been made beloved to me."
(Sunan al-Nasa'i 3940)

Women deserve the utmost kindness, especially in the case of
marriage, since a woman makes many a great sacrifice for the
sake of marriage, starting from her leaving her own home and
family to move in with another person and start a completely
new family. The husband should be very considerate towards his
wife as it is unlikely the husband would have been able to make
such changes to his live for someone else.

12

حَدَّثَنَا عُبَيْدُ بْنُ إِسْمَاعِيلَ، حَدَّثَنَا أَبُو أُسَامَةَ، عَنْ هِشَامٍ، عَنْ أَبِيهِ، عَنْ عَائِشَةَ رَضِيَ اللَّهُ عَنْهَا، قَالَتْ: قَالَ لِي رَسُولُ اللَّهِ صَلَّى اللَّهُ عَلَيْهِ وَسَلَّمَ: إِنِّي لَأَعْلَمُ إِذَا كُنْتِ عَنِّي رَاضِيَةً، وَإِذَا كُنْتِ عَلَيَّ غَضْبَى قَالَتْ: فَقُلْتُ: مِنْ أَيْنَ تَعْرِفُ ذَلِكَ؟ فَقَالَ: أَمَّا إِذَا كُنْتِ عَنِّي رَاضِيَةً، فَإِنَّكِ تَقُولِينَ: لَا وَرَبِّ مُحَمَّدٍ، وَإِذَا كُنْتِ عَلَيَّ غَضْبَى، قُلْتِ: لَا وَرَبِّ إِبْرَاهِيمَ قَالَتْ: قُلْتُ: أَجَلْ وَاللَّهِ يَا رَسُولَ اللَّهِ، مَا أَهْجُرُ إِلَّا اسْمَكَ

~ Hadīth 7 ~

TO SENSE SPOUSE'S FEELINGS

Narrated by 'Aisha:
The Messenger of Allah ﷺ said to her, "I know
when you are pleased with me or angry with me." I
said, "How do you know that?" He said, "When you
are pleased with me, you say, 'No, by the Lord of
Muhammad,' but when you are angry with me, then
you say, 'No, by the Lord of Abraham.' " I said, "Yes
(you are right), but by Allah, O Allah's Messenger, I
leave nothing but your name."

Sahih al-Bukhari 5228

Notes: The spouse should try to recognise and respond to the
feelings of one's spouse as this shows care and compassion. The
Prophet ﷺ would be considerate such that if he saw his wives
were upset then he would try to comfort and console them, this
can seen in the following *hadith* where he ﷺ wiped away his
wife's tears and comforted her;

فَجَعَلَ رَسُولُ اللهِ صَلَّى اللهُ عَلَيْهِ وَسَلَّمَ يَمْسَحُ بِيَدَيْهِ عَيْنَيْهَا وُيُسْكِتُهَا

*Safiyya was on journey with the prophet ﷺ and she was late and
crying, the prophet ﷺ wiped her tears with his hands and tried to stop
her crying.* (Sunan al-Kubra of lil-Nasai 9117)

It is important that one also needs to understand that their
spouses are not psychic, they cannot read minds nor know what
is inside the hearts. Sometimes it helps to tell them and talk to
them. Talking about each other's problems is a good way to
open up and build trust, as well as helping towards an engaging
relationship.

الحديث الثامن

حَدَّثَنَا أَبُو كُرَيْبٍ، وَمُوسَى بْنُ حِزَامٍ،

قَالَا: حَدَّثَنَا حُسَيْنُ بْنُ عَلِيٍّ، عَنْ

زَائِدَةَ، عَنْ مَيْسَرَةَ الْأَشْجَعِيِّ، عَنْ أَبِي

حَازِمٍ، عَنْ أَبِي هُرَيْرَةَ رَضِيَ اللَّهُ عَنْهُ،

قَالَ: قَالَ رَسُولُ اللَّهِ صَلَّى اللَّهُ عَلَيْهِ

وَسَلَّمَ: اسْتَوْصُوا بِالنِّسَاءِ، فَإِنَّ الْمَرْأَةَ

خُلِقَتْ مِنْ ضِلَعٍ، وَإِنَّ أَعْوَجَ شَيْءٍ

فِي الضِّلَعِ أَعْلَاهُ، فَإِنْ ذَهَبْتَ تُقِيمُهُ

كَسَرْتَهُ، وَإِنْ تَرَكْتَهُ لَمْ يَزَلْ أَعْوَجَ،

فَاسْتَوْصُوا بِالنِّسَاءِ

~ *Hadīth 8* ~

RESPECTING SPOUSE'S NATURE

Narrated by Abu Huraira:
The Messenger of Allah ﷺ said, "Treat women nicely,
for a woman is created from a rib, and the most curved
portion of the rib is its upper portion, so, if you should
try to straighten it; it will break, but if you leave it as it
is, it will remain curved. So treat women nicely."

Sahih al-Bukhari 3331

Notes: Allah has created men and women from each other, yet
they are completely different in many aspects. The spouses may
not understand each other, but they need to respect each other's
differences. One should not expect their spouse to change their
nature so long as this is not contrary to the *shariah*. Like a rib,
(the function of which is to be curved) this is not a fault and a
weakness, rather it is the nature of the rib and serves its own
purpose and any change to it will not allow it to function and
it will become obsolete. Thus the Prophet ﷺ elaborates and
mentions that if you wish to live with them and benefit from them
then benefit from them as they are, do not try to change them:

فَإِنِ اسْتَمْتَعْتَ بِهَا اسْتَمْتَعْتَ بِهَا وَبِهَا عِوَجٌ

"So if you wish to benefit by her, benefit by her while crookedness
remains in her." (Sahih Muslim 1467)

But if you try to change their nature ,then the consequences will
lead to difficulty and not be able to live with each other.

وَإِنْ ذَهَبْتَ تُقِيمُهَا كَسَرْتَهَا وَكَسْرُهَا طَلَاقُهَا

"And if you attempt to straighten her, you will break her, and breaking
her means divorcing her." (Sahih Muslim 1467)

16

الحديث التاسع

وَحَدَّثَنِي إِبْرَاهِيمُ بْنُ مُوسَى الرَّازِيُّ،
حَدَّثَنَا عِيسَى يَعْنِي ابْنَ يُونُسَ، حَدَّثَنَا
عَبْدُ الْحَمِيدِ بْنُ جَعْفَرٍ، عَنْ عِمْرَانَ
بْنِ أَبِي أَنَسٍ، عَنْ عُمَرَ بْنِ الْحَكَمِ،
عَنْ أَبِي هُرَيْرَةَ، قَالَ: قَالَ رَسُولُ اللهِ
صَلَّى اللهُ عَلَيْهِ وَسَلَّمَ
لَا يَفْرَكْ مُؤْمِنٌ مُؤْمِنَةً، إِنْ كَرِهَ مِنْهَا
خُلُقًا رَضِيَ مِنْهَا آخَرَ

~ Hadīth 9 ~

NOT TO DISLIKE ONE'S SPOUSE

Narrated by Abu Huraira:
The Messenger of Allah ﷺ said, "A believing man
should not hate a believing woman (his wife); if he
dislikes one of her characteristics, then he will be
pleased with another."

Sahih Muslim 1469

Notes: Marriage is a union of two different individuals and two
souls, each spouse with their own life experiences. This often
leads to a spouse expecting the other to have the same likes,
dislikes and preferences which can cause disagreement and
disputes. There may be traits that one might not like in their
spouse but the Prophetic teaching is to overlook the few faults
and look at the many good traits of the spouse, Allah says:

وَعَاشِرُوهُنَّ بِالْمَعْرُوفِ. فَإِن كَرِهْتُمُوهُنَّ فَعَسَىٰ أَن تَكْرَهُوا شَيْئًا وَيَجْعَلَ اللَّهُ فِيهِ خَيْرًا كَثِيرًا

"And live with them in kindness. For if you dislike them; perhaps you
dislike a thing and Allah places therein much good."

(Al-Quran s4 v19)

One should look at and appreciate these good traits, as
appreciating one's spouse can lead to a much happier
atmosphere. The Prophet ﷺ said:

مَنْ لَمْ يَشْكُرِ النَّاسَ لَمْ يَشْكُرِ اللَّهَ

"Whoever does not show gratitude to people is not grateful to Allah."

(Jami` at-Tirmidhi 1955)

الحديث العاشر

حَدَّثَنَا بَكْرُ بْنُ خَلَفٍ، حَدَّثَنَا أَبُو عَاصِمٍ، عَنْ جَعْفَرِ بْنِ يَحْيَى بْنِ ثَوْبَانَ، عَنْ عَمِّهِ عُمَارَةَ بْنِ ثَوْبَانَ، عَنْ عَطَاءٍ، عَنِ ابْنِ عَبَّاسٍ، أَنَّ النَّبِيَّ صَلَّى اللهُ عَلَيْهِ وَسَلَّمَ، قَالَ: لَا تَسْأَلُ الْمَرْأَةُ زَوْجَهَا الطَّلَاقَ فِي غَيْرِ كُنْهِهِ فَتَجِدَ رِيحَ الْجَنَّةِ، وَإِنَّ رِيحَهَا لَيُوجَدُ مِنْ مَسِيرَةِ أَرْبَعِينَ عَامًا

~ *Hadīth 10* ~

NOT TO GIVE UP ON ONE'S SPOUSE

Narrated by Ibn 'Abbas:
The Prophet ﷺ said: "No woman asks for divorce when it is not absolutely necessary, but she will never smell the fragrance of paradise, although its fragrance can be detected from a distance of forty years' travel."

Sunan Ibn Majah 2054

Notes: While Islam allows divorce as a means of seperation for the couple who despite sufficient efforts cannot come to a mutual reconciliation, yet it is considered to be the worst of permissible actions and should not be taken lightly.

Divorcing a spouse because one cannot come to terms with someone who is different is a great fault on our side. The Prophet ﷺ mentions the severity of this;

أَبْغَضُ الْحَلَالِ إِلَى اللَّهِ الطَّلَاقُ

"The most hated of halal things to Allah, is divorce. "
(Sunan Ibn Majah 2018)

Marriage is a commitment that requires dedication, patience and perseverance especially in the early stages of marriage as this is the time when there is often a clash of the spouse's characters. To use divorce as a quick getaway is a fault on our part and acting in such way will lead us to always run away form the slightest difficulties and challenges in life and in turn earn the anger of Allah.

الحديث الحادي عشر

حَدَّثَنَا إِسْحَاقُ بْنُ إِبْرَاهِيمَ الْحَنْظَلِيُّ، عَنْ عِيسَى، عَنِ الْأَوْزَاعِيِّ، عَنِ الزُّهْرِيِّ، عَنْ عُرْوَةَ، عَنْ عَائِشَةَ رَضِيَ اللَّهُ عَنْهَا، قَالَتْ: رَأَيْتُ النَّبِيَّ صَلَّى اللَّهُ عَلَيْهِ وَسَلَّمَ يَسْتُرُنِي بِرِدَائِهِ، وَأَنَا أَنْظُرُ إِلَى الْحَبَشَةِ يَلْعَبُونَ فِي الْمَسْجِدِ، حَتَّى أَكُونَ أَنَا الَّتِي أَسْأَمُ، فَاقْدُرُوا قَدْرَ الْجَارِيَةِ الْحَدِيثَةِ السِّنِّ، الْحَرِيصَةِ عَلَى اللَّهْوِ

~ *Hadīth 11* ~

BE CONSIDERATE TOWARDS SPOUSE

Narrated by 'Aisha:
The Prophet ﷺ was shielding me with his cloak
while I was watching the display by Ethiopians in the
courtyard of the masjid. I continued watching till I was
satisfied. So you should understand the eagerness of
young girls to watch such sports.

Sahih al-Bukhari 5236

Notes: One should pay extra attention and consideration to the
likes, dislikes and emotional needs of their spouse. In this *hadith*
the Prophet ﷺ was considerate towards his wife, such that to
accommodate her interest, he stood idle for a lengthy period of
time covering her until his wife was satisfied and became bored.
In another *hadith* it mentions that the Prophet ﷺ would bring
along the friends of his wife so that they could enjoy each other's
company;

"فَكَانَ يُسَرِّبُ إِلَيَّ صَوَاحِبَاتِي يُلاَعِبْنَنِي"
"He used to bring my friends to me to play with me."
(Sunan Ibn Majah 1982)

It is good for spouses to have their own friends and sometimes
enjoy their company, but this should not lead to their spouse
being neglected, as this will then become a problem in
their marriage and hinder any bond, since the friends will
automatically occupy a big part of one's life leaving little room
for their spouse. The marital relationship should be prioritised
especially in the early stages.

الحديث الثاني عشر

حَدَّثَنَا إِسْحَاقُ بْنُ إِبْرَاهِيمَ، حَدَّثَنَا
عَبْدَةُ، حَدَّثَنَا هِشَامُ بْنُ عُرْوَةَ، عَنْ
أَبِيهِ، عَنْ عَائِشَةَ، رَضِيَ اللَّهُ عَنْهَا
قَالَتْ: هَلَكَتْ قِلَادَةٌ لِأَسْمَاءَ، فَبَعَثَ
النَّبِيُّ صَلَّى اللَّهُ عَلَيْهِ وَسَلَّمَ فِي طَلَبِهَا
رِجَالًا، فَحَضَرَتِ الصَّلَاةُ وَلَيْسُوا عَلَى
وُضُوءٍ، وَلَمْ يَجِدُوا مَاءً، فَصَلَّوْا وَهُمْ
عَلَى غَيْرِ وُضُوءٍ، فَذَكَرُوا ذَلِكَ لِلنَّبِيِّ
صَلَّى اللَّهُ عَلَيْهِ وَسَلَّمَ، فَأَنْزَلَ اللَّهُ آيَةَ
التَّيَمُّمِ زَادَ ابْنُ نُمَيْرٍ، عَنْ هِشَامٍ، عَنْ
أَبِيهِ، عَنْ عَائِشَةَ: اسْتَعَارَتْ مِنْ أَسْمَاءَ

~ *Hadīth 12* ~

GOING OUT OF THE WAY FOR ONE'S SPOUSE

Narrated 'Aisha:
A necklace belonging to Asma' was lost, and the
Prophet ﷺ sent men in its search. The time for the
prayer became due and they were without ablution
and they could not find water; therefore they prayed
without ablution. They mentioned this to the Prophet
ﷺ. Then Allah revealed the Verse of *Tayammum*. ('Aisha
added: that she had borrowed the necklace from
Asma').

Sahih al-Bukhari 5882

Notes: In this hadith the wife of the Prophet ﷺ lost a necklace
she borrowed while on a journey, the Prophet ﷺ stopped the
whole caravan and sent people to search for it. One needs to
be patient and understanding and at times will have to make
sacrifices for one's spouse. We should do this without hesitation
and not expect a favour in return. One often expects their
spouses to be good, righteous, pious and caring individuals,
but remember, it is oneself who needs to make one's own
contribution towards creating a healthy and flourishing marriage.
Whatever good that one does to their spouse, they should not
expect any reward from them, as not receiving acknowledgment
from them can lead to disappointment. Rather one should expect
the reward from Allah. Allah says:

مَنْ عَمِلَ صَالِحًا مِّن ذَكَرٍ أَوْ أُنثَىٰ وَهُوَ مُؤْمِنٌ فَلَنُحْيِيَنَّهُ حَيَاةً طَيِّبَةً وَلَنَجْزِيَنَّهُمْ أَجْرَهُم بِأَحْسَنِ
مَا كَانُوا يَعْمَلُونَ

"Whoever does righteousness, whether male or female, while they are
a believer - We will surely cause them to live a good life, and We will
surely give them their reward [in the Hereafter] according to the best of
what they used to do." (Al-Quran s16 v97)

24

الحديث الثالث عشر

حَدَّثَنَا إِسْمَاعِيلُ، قَالَ: حَدَّثَنِي سُلَيْمَانُ بْنُ بِلَالٍ، قَالَ: قَالَ هِشَامُ بْنُ عُرْوَةَ: أَخْبَرَنِي أَبِي، عَنْ عَائِشَةَ رَضِيَ اللَّهُ عَنْهَا، قَالَتْ: دَخَلَ عَبْدُ الرَّحْمَنِ بْنُ أَبِي بَكْرٍ وَمَعَهُ سِوَاكٌ يَسْتَنُّ بِهِ، فَنَظَرَ إِلَيْهِ رَسُولُ اللَّهِ صَلَّى اللَّهُ عَلَيْهِ وَسَلَّمَ، فَقُلْتُ لَهُ: أَعْطِنِي هَذَا السِّوَاكَ يَا عَبْدَ الرَّحْمَنِ، فَأَعْطَانِيهِ، فَقَصَمْتُهُ، ثُمَّ مَضَغْتُهُ فَأَعْطَيْتُهُ رَسُولَ اللَّهِ صَلَّى اللَّهُ عَلَيْهِ وَسَلَّمَ، فَاسْتَنَّ بِهِ وَهُوَ مُسْتَسْنِدٌ إِلَى صَدْرِي

~ *Hadīth 13* ~

GIVING GIFTS TO ONE'S SPOUSE

Narrated by `Aisha:
`Abdur-Rahman bin Abi Bakr came holding a *miswak* with which he was cleaning his teeth. Allah's Messenger ﷺ looked at him. I requested `Abdur-Rahman to give the *miswak* to me and after he gave it to me I divided it, chewed it and gave it to the Messenger of Allah ﷺ. Then he cleaned his teeth with it while he was resting against my chest.

Sahih al-Bukhari 890

Notes: In a healthy marriage one should try to be conscious of the likes and dislikes of their spouse, and make an effort to accommodate their preferences. A simple way to build marital bond is to get each other small gifts, which would show that one has thought about the other. The Prophet ﷺ would encourage exchanging gifts. It can build mutual love and respect, it can a token of appreciation or even a symbol of apology as he ﷺ has said that exchanging gifts removes hard feelings for each other in one's hearts:

تَهَادَوْا فَإِنَّ الهَدِيَّةَ تُذْهِبُ وَحَرَ الصَّدْرِ

"Exchange gifts, for indeed the gift removes bad feelings from the heart." (Jami` at-Tirmidhi 2130)

As seen from this *hadith*, one can gift their spouse something as simple as a *miswak* (natural toothbrush) which despite being very small carries great reward as the Prophet ﷺ said:

السِّوَاكُ مَطْهَرَةٌ لِلْفَمِ مَرْضَاةٌ لِلرَّبِّ

"Siwak purifies the mouth and is pleasing to the Lord."

(Sunan al-Nasai 5)

الحديث الرابع عشر

حَدَّثَنَا وَاصِلُ بْنُ عَبْدِ الأَعْلَى قَالَ:
حَدَّثَنَا مُحَمَّدُ بْنُ فُضَيْلٍ، عَنْ عَبْدِ
اللَّهِ بْنِ عَبْدِ الرَّحْمَنِ أَبِي نَصْرٍ، عَنْ
مُسَاوِرٍ الحِمْيَرِيِّ، عَنْ أُمِّهِ، عَنْ أُمِّ
سَلَمَةَ قَالَتْ: قَالَ رَسُولُ اللَّهِ صَلَّى اللَّهُ
عَلَيْهِ وَسَلَّمَ
أَيُّمَا امْرَأَةٍ مَاتَتْ وَزَوْجُهَا عَنْهَا رَاضٍ
دَخَلَتِ الجَنَّةَ

~ Hadīth 14 ~

BEING PLEASED WITH ONE'S SPOUSE

Narrated by Umm Salamah:
The Messenger of Allah ﷺ said: "Any woman who dies while her husband is pleased with her, shall enter Paradise".

Jami' al-Timidhi 1161

Notes: One should always try to appreciate and show pleasure at the efforts made by the spouse. They might have gone through much thinking and sacrifice for something you might deem insignificant. Try to express your pleasure at things they do for you, as this can be a means of happiness and satisfaction for them and will boost their moral. The Prophet ﷺ has given great significance on the spouses being pleased with each other with a promise of a great reward:

إِذَا صَلَّتِ الْمَرْأَةُ خَمْسَهَا، وَصَامَتْ شَهْرَهَا، وَحَفِظَتْ فَرْجَهَا، وَأَطَاعَتْ زَوْجَهَا قِيلَ لَهَا: ادْخُلِي الْجَنَّةَ مِنْ أَيِّ أَبْوَابِ الْجَنَّةِ شِئْتِ

"Any woman who offers her five daily prayers, fasts Ramadan, guards her chastity and obeys her husband, can enter Paradise by whichever of the doors she wishes." (Musnad Ahmad 1661)

One should also make dua for one's spouse as this will build mutual love. The Prophet ﷺ made dua for his wife:

اللَّهُمَّ اغْفِرْ لِعَائِشَةَ مَا تَقَدَّمَ مِنْ ذَنبِهَا وَمَا تَأَخَّرَ مَا أَسَرَّتْ وَمَا أَعْلَنَتْ

"O Allah, forgive 'Aisha for her past and future sins, in secret and in public." (Sahih Ibn Hibban 7111)

الحديث الخامس عشر

حَدَّثَنَا آدَمُ، قَالَ: حَدَّثَنَا شُعْبَةُ، قَالَ:
حَدَّثَنَا الْحَكَمُ، عَنْ إِبْرَاهِيمَ، عَنِ
الْأَسْوَدِ، قَالَ: سَأَلْتُ عَائِشَةَ مَا كَانَ
النَّبِيُّ صَلَّى اللهُ عَلَيْهِ وَسَلَّمَ
يَصْنَعُ فِي بَيْتِهِ؟ قَالَتْ
كَانَ يَكُونُ فِي مِهْنَةِ أَهْلِهِ
تَعْنِي خِدْمَةَ أَهْلِهِ
فَإِذَا حَضَرَتِ الصَّلَاةُ خَرَجَ إِلَى الصَّلَاةِ

~ *Hadīth 15* ~

HELPING SPOUSE WITH CHORES

Narrated by Al-Aswad:
That he asked `Aisha "What did the Prophet ﷺ used to
do in his house?" She replied, "He used to keep himself
busy serving his family and when it was the time for
prayer he would leave."

Sahih al-Bukhari 676

Notes: The Prophet ﷺ was one of the busiest of people with
the responsibilty of the *ummah* and guidance for the whole of
humanity. Yet when he was at home, he would actively help with
the household chores. Helping one's wife in the house allows
opportunity to spend quality time together as well as develops
productivity.

In another *hadith* it mentions that he ﷺ would repair his own
shoes as well as patch his own clothing:

كَانَ رَسُولُ اللهِ صَلَّى اللهُ عَلَيْهِ وَسَلَّمَ يَخْصِفُ نَعْلَهُ، وَيَخِيطُ ثَوْبَهُ،
وَيَعْمَلُ فِي بَيْتِهِ كَمَا يَعْمَلُ أَحَدُكُمْ فِي بَيْتِهِ

*"The Prophet ﷺ would repair his shoes, patch his clothing and do
household chores like any of you does at your homes."*

(Musnad Ahmad 25341)

Marriage is a relationship of mutual bond and it needs mutual
co-operation for a relationship to flourish. A little sign of support,
effort and appreciation improves love and mutual respect for
each other.

الحديث السادس عشر

حَدَّثَنَا عَبْدُ اللَّهِ بْنُ يُوسُفَ، أَخْبَرَنَا اللَّيْثُ،
قَالَ: حَدَّثَنِي عُقَيْلٌ، عَنِ ابْنِ شِهَابٍ،
قَالَ: سَمِعْتُ أَبَا سَلَمَةَ، قَالَ: أَخْبَرَنِي جَابِرُ
بْنُ عَبْدِ اللَّهِ رَضِيَ اللَّهُ عَنْهُمَا، أَنَّهُ سَمِعَ
النَّبِيَّ صَلَّى اللَّهُ عَلَيْهِ وَسَلَّمَ، يَقُولُ: " ثُمَّ
فَتَرَ عَنِّي الْوَحْيُ فَتْرَةً، فَبَيْنَا أَنَا أَمْشِي،
سَمِعْتُ صَوْتًا مِنَ السَّمَاءِ، فَرَفَعْتُ بَصَرِي
قِبَلَ السَّمَاءِ، فَإِذَا الْمَلَكُ الَّذِي جَاءَنِي
بِحِرَاءٍ، قَاعِدٌ عَلَى كُرْسِيٍّ بَيْنَ السَّمَاءِ
وَالْأَرْضِ، فَجُئِثْتُ مِنْهُ، حَتَّى هَوَيْتُ إِلَى
الْأَرْضِ، فَجِئْتُ أَهْلِي فَقُلْتُ: زَمِّلُونِي
زَمِّلُونِي، فَأَنْزَلَ اللَّهُ تَعَالَى {يَا أَيُّهَا الْمُدَّثِّرُ
قُمْ فَأَنْذِرْ} إِلَى قَوْلِهِ {وَالرُّجْزَ} فَاهْجُرْ
"، قَالَ أَبُو سَلَمَةَ: وَالرُّجْزُ: الْأَوْثَانُ

صحيح البخاري ٣٢٣٨

~ *Hadīth 16* ~

COMFORTING ONE'S SPOUSE

Narrated by Jabir bin `Abdullah:
He heard the Prophet ﷺ saying, "Revelation was
delayed for a short period but suddenly, as I was
walking, I heard a voice in the sky: When I looked up,
to my surprise, I saw the angel who had come to me in
the Cave Hira, and he was sitting on a chair in between
the sky and the earth. I was so frightened by him that
I fell on the ground and came to my wife and said,
'Cover me! , cover me!' Then Allah sent the Revelation:
*"O, You wrapped up! Arise and warn! And your Lord
magnify And keep pure your garments, And abandon the
idols."* (s74 v1-5)

Sahih al-Bukhari 3238

Notes: This hadith beautifully shows how the Prophet ﷺ sought
comfort in his wife at his moment of distress, such that he was
fearful for his life and ran home straight to his wife. Any healthy
marriage needs that the spouses find comfort in each other, they
should be there for each other at the moment of need when one
suffers a calamity or a loss in life or any situation of distress. The
last thing that a spouse in distress wishes to hear is something
like "I told you so" etc.
One should show compassion for the loss and distress of one's
spouse, doing so will cause Allah to become compassionate
towards us. The Prophet ﷺ mentions (regarding being
compassionate):

الرَّاحِمُونَ يَرْحَمُهُمُ الرَّحْمَنُ ارْحَمُوا أَهْلَ الأَرْضِ يَرْحَمْكُمْ مَنْ فِي السَّمَاءِ

*"The merciful ones are shown mercy by Ar-Rahman. Be merciful on the
earth, and you will be shown mercy from Who is above the heavens."*

(Jami` al-Tirmidhi 1924)

الحديث السابع عشر

حَدَّثَنَا إِسْحَاقُ بْنُ مَنْصُورٍ، وَعَبْدُ بْنُ حُمَيْدٍ، قَالَا: أَخْبَرَنَا عَبْدُ الرَّزَّاقِ قَالَ: أَخْبَرَنَا مَعْمَرٌ، عَنْ ثَابِتٍ، عَنْ أَنَسٍ، قَالَ: بَلَغَ صَفِيَّةَ أَنَّ حَفْصَةَ، قَالَتْ: بِنْتُ يَهُودِيٍّ، فَبَكَتْ، فَدَخَلَ عَلَيْهَا النَّبِيُّ صَلَّى اللَّهُ عَلَيْهِ وَسَلَّمَ وَهِيَ تَبْكِي، فَقَالَ: مَا يُبْكِيكِ ؟ فَقَالَتْ: قَالَتْ لِي حَفْصَةُ: إِنِّي بِنْتُ يَهُودِيٍّ، فَقَالَ النَّبِيُّ

~ *Hadīth 17* ~

MOTIVATING ONE'S SPOUSE

Narrated by Anas:
"It reached Safiyyah that Hafsa said: 'The daughter of
a Jew' so she wept. Then the Prophet ﷺ came to her
while she was crying, and asked; 'What makes you
cry?' She said: 'Hafsa referred to me as the daughter
of a Jew.' So the Prophet ﷺ said: 'And you are also a
daughter of a Prophet, and your uncle is a Prophet, and
you are married to a Prophet, so what is she boasting to
you about?' Then he said: 'Fear Allah, O Hafsa.'"

Jami' al-Tirmidhi 3894

Notes: Motivating one's spouse is a crucial part of a harmonious
marital relationship. One's spouse may feel upset and
demoralised due to pressure from other aspects of their lives,
thus having someone at home who will encourage, motivate and
inspire is what one should expect and needs from their spouse.
This can be seen in the following hadith where Khadija comforted
and motivated the Prophet ﷺ when he doubted his own sanity:

فَقَالَتْ خَدِيجَةُ كَلَّا وَاللَّهِ مَا يُخْزِيكَ اللَّهُ أَبَدًا، إِنَّكَ لَتَصِلُ الرَّحِمَ، وَتَحْمِلُ الْكَلَّ، وَتَكْسِبُ
الْمَعْدُومَ، وَتَقْرِي الضَّيْفَ، وَتُعِينُ عَلَى نَوَائِبِ الْحَقِّ

*"Never! By Allah, Allah will never disgrace you. You keep good
relations with you kin, help the poor and the destitute, serve your guests
generously and assist those afflicted by calamities."*
(Sahih Muslim 160)

الحديث الثامن عشر

حَدَّثَنَا مُحَمَّدُ بْنُ بَشَّارٍ قَالَ: حَدَّثَنَا أَبُو أَحْمَدَ الزُّبَيْرِيُّ قَالَ: حَدَّثَنَا سُفْيَانُ، ح وَحَدَّثَنَا مَحْمُودُ بْنُ غَيْلَانَ قَالَ: حَدَّثَنَا بِشْرُ بْنُ السَّرِيِّ، وَأَبُو أَحْمَدَ قَالَا: حَدَّثَنَا سُفْيَانُ، عَنْ عَبْدِ اللَّهِ بْنِ عُثْمَانَ بْنِ خُثَيْمٍ، عَنْ شَهْرِ بْنِ حَوْشَبٍ، عَنْ أَسْمَاءَ بِنْتِ يَزِيدَ قَالَتْ: قَالَ رَسُولُ اللَّهِ صَلَّى اللَّهُ عَلَيْهِ وَسَلَّمَ: لَا يَحِلُّ الْكَذِبُ إِلَّا فِي ثَلَاثٍ: يُحَدِّثُ الرَّجُلُ امْرَأَتَهُ لِيُرْضِيَهَا، وَالْكَذِبُ فِي الْحَرْبِ، وَالْكَذِبُ لِيُصْلِحَ بَيْنَ النَّاسِ

~ Hadīth 18 ~

MAKING SPOUSE FEEL GOOD

Narrated by Asma bint Yazid:
The Messenger of Allah ﷺ said. "It is not lawful to lie except in three cases: When a man lies to his wife to please her, to lie during war, and to lie in order to bring peace between the people."

Jami` at-Tirmidhi 1939

Notes: Islam places great significance on truthfulness and prohibits lying. The Prophet ﷺ says:

إِنَّ الصِّدْقَ يَهْدِي إِلَى الْبِرِّ وَإِنَّ الْبِرَّ يَهْدِي إِلَى الْجَنَّةِ وَإِنَّ الرَّجُلَ لَيَصْدُقُ حَتَّى يُكْتَبَ صِدِّيقًا وَإِنَّ الْكَذِبَ يَهْدِي إِلَى الْفُجُورِ وَإِنَّ الْفُجُورَ يَهْدِي إِلَى النَّارِ وَإِنَّ الرَّجُلَ لَيَكْذِبُ حَتَّى يُكْتَبَ كَذَّابًا

"Surely truth leads to virtue, which leads one to Paradise and a person tells the truth until he is recorded as truthful. Lie leads to obscenity and obscenity leads to Hell, and a person tells a lie until he is recorded as a liar." (Sahih Muslim 2607)

Sometimes being lenient with the truth in trivial matters can help build love and secure marital bond. Just say, one of the spouse bought a gift or cooked something for the other, if they say that they don't like it or it does not taste good then this may hurt the feelings of their spouse and they may feel that their effort was in vain. Therefore in such instances one can say something contrary to the truth to make one's spouse feel good about themselves.

الحديث التاسع عشر

أَخْبَرَنِي أَحْمَدُ بْنُ يُوسُفَ الْمُهَلَّبِيُّ النَّيْسَابُورِيُّ، حَدَّثَنَا عُمَرُ بْنُ عَبْدِ اللَّهِ بْنِ رَزِينٍ، حَدَّثَنَا سُفْيَانُ بْنُ حُسَيْنٍ، عَنْ دَاوُدَ الْوَرَّاقِ، عَنْ سَعِيدِ بْنِ حَكِيمِ بْنِ مُعَاوِيَةَ، عَنْ أَبِيهِ، عَنْ جَدِّهِ مُعَاوِيَةَ الْقُشَيْرِيِّ، قَالَ: أَتَيْتُ رَسُولَ اللَّهِ صَلَّى اللَّهُ عَلَيْهِ وَسَلَّمَ، قَالَ: فَقُلْتُ: مَا تَقُولُ: فِي نِسَائِنَا قَالَ: أَطْعِمُوهُنَّ مِمَّا تَأْكُلُونَ، وَاكْسُوهُنَّ مِمَّا تَكْتَسُونَ، وَلَا تَضْرِبُوهُنَّ، وَلَا تُقَبِّحُوهُنَّ

~ Hadīth 19 ~

TREATING SPOUSE AS ONESELF

Narrated by Mu'awiyah al-Qushayri:
I went to the Messenger of Allah ﷺ and asked him:
"What do you command about our wives?" He replied:
"Feed them what you eat yourself, and clothe them
(similar quality) to what you clothe yourself, and do
not hit them nor abuse them."

Sunan Abi Dawud 2144

Notes: Islam allows everyone to live their lives according to
their wealth and according to what Allah has bestowed upon
them without extravagance and boastfulness. Likewise our
spouse should have similar to what we ourselves eat, wear
and use. A marriage needs the spouses to have the sense of
sharing; sharing in each others happiness as well as sharing in
each other's hardship. Likewise they will share and be there for
each other in abundance or poverty. It is through fairness and
sharing that there will be balance, justice and harmony in the
household. Without this there is only room left for jealousy and
envy, inevitably leading to spouses despising each other. Also, in
a harmonious marriage the spouses should consult each other as
mentioned in the hadith:

فَقَالَتْ أُمُّ سَلَمَةَ: يَا نَبِيَّ اللَّهِ، أَتُحِبُّ ذَلِكَ، اخْرُجْ ثُمَّ لَا تُكَلِّمْ أَحَدًا مِنْهُمْ كَلِمَةً، حَتَّى تَنْحَرَ
بُدْنَكَ، وَتَدْعُوَ حَالِقَكَ فَيَحْلِقَكَ، فَخَرَجَ فَلَمْ يُكَلِّمْ أَحَدًا مِنْهُمْ حَتَّى فَعَلَ ذَلِكَ

*Umm Salama said, "O the Prophet of Allah! Do you want your order to
be carried out? Go out and do not say a word to anybody till you have
slaughtered your sacrifice and call your barber to shave your head." So,
the Prophet ﷺ went out and did not talk to anyone of them till he did
that."* (Sahih al-Bukhari 2731)

الحَدِيثُ العِشْرُونَ

وحَدَّثَنِي زُهَيْرُ بْنُ حَرْبٍ، حَدَّثَنَا يَزِيدُ بْنُ هَارُونَ، أَخْبَرَنَا حَمَّادُ بْنُ سَلَمَةَ، عَنْ ثَابِتٍ، عَنْ أَنَسٍ، أَنَّ جَارًا لِرَسُولِ اللهِ صَلَّى اللهُ عَلَيْهِ وَسَلَّمَ فَارِسِيًّا كَانَ طَيِّبَ الْمَرَقِ، فَصَنَعَ لِرَسُولِ اللهِ صَلَّى اللهُ عَلَيْهِ وَسَلَّمَ، ثُمَّ جَاءَ يَدْعُوهُ، فَقَالَ: وَهَذِهِ؟ لِعَائِشَةَ، فَقَالَ: لَا، فَقَالَ رَسُولُ اللهِ صَلَّى اللهُ عَلَيْهِ وَسَلَّمَ: لَا ، فَعَادَ يَدْعُوهُ، فَقَالَ رَسُولُ اللهِ صَلَّى اللهُ عَلَيْهِ وَسَلَّمَ: وَهَذِهِ؟ ، قَالَ: لَا، قَالَ رَسُولُ اللهِ صَلَّى اللهُ عَلَيْهِ وَسَلَّمَ: لَا ، ثُمَّ عَادَ يَدْعُوهُ، فَقَالَ رَسُولُ اللهِ صَلَّى اللهُ عَلَيْهِ وَسَلَّمَ: وَهَذِهِ؟ ، قَالَ: نَعَمْ فِي الثَّالِثَةِ، فَقَامَا يَتَدَافَعَانِ حَتَّى أَتَيَا مَنْزِلَهُ

~ *Hadīth 20* ~

EATING WITH ONE'S SPOUSE

Narrated by Anas:
The Messenger of Allah ﷺ had a Persian neighbour who was good at making soup. He prepared soup for the Prophet ﷺ and came to invite him. He ﷺ said, 'A'isha is also here (if he would also invite her). He said, no. Thereupon the Prophet ﷺ declined the offer. He returned inviting him, and Prophet ﷺ said, she is also here. He said, no. Thereupon Prophet ﷺ again declined the offer. He returned again to invite him and Prophet ﷺ again said, she is also here. He (the host) said: "Yes" on the third time. Then he ﷺ accepted his invitation, and both of them set out to his house.

Sahih Muslim 2037

Notes: This hadith shows the effort and sacrifice the Prophet ﷺ was willing to make in order to spend time and eat with his wife. He declined an invitation for a food item that he likes and preferred the company of his wife. It is these small gestures, sacrifices and choices one makes, and the priority that one gives to their marriage that plays a huge impact in cultivating the love and respect to develop the bond between the hearts.
In this modern day with mass communication, mass production and fast food; it is easy to find food anywhere and everywhere. Due to this it is quite rare for the spouses to get an opportunity to eat together and spend that time together. From this *hadith* we can see that the Prophet ﷺ despite having the opportunity to go alone; chose to spend that time with his wife.

الحديث الحادي و العشرون

حَدَّثَنَا أَبُو بَكْرِ بْنُ أَبِي شَيْبَةَ، وَزُهَيْرُ بْنُ حَرْبٍ، قَالَا: حَدَّثَنَا وَكِيعٌ، عَنْ مِسْعَرٍ، وَسُفْيَانَ، عَنِ الْمِقْدَامِ بْنِ شُرَيْحٍ، عَنْ أَبِيهِ، عَنْ عَائِشَةَ قَالَتْ: كُنْتُ أَشْرَبُ وَأَنَا حَائِضٌ، ثُمَّ أُنَاوِلُهُ النَّبِيَّ صَلَّى اللهُ عَلَيْهِ وَسَلَّمَ فَيَضَعُ فَاهُ عَلَى مَوْضِعِ فِيَّ، فَيَشْرَبُ، وَأَتَعَرَّقُ الْعَرْقَ وَأَنَا حَائِضٌ، ثُمَّ أُنَاوِلُهُ النَّبِيَّ صَلَّى اللهُ عَلَيْهِ وَسَلَّمَ فَيَضَعُ فَاهُ عَلَى مَوْضِعِ فِيَّ

~ *Hadīth 21* ~

SHARING FOOD WITH ONE'S SPOUSE

Narrated by 'A'isha:
"While menstruating, I would drink from a cup and
I would pass the cup to the Prophet ﷺ and he would
drink by placing his lips where mine had been.
While menstruating, I would bite meat on the bone and
I would pass it over to the Prophet ﷺ and he would
bite on the same place I had placed my mouth."

Sahih Muslim 300

Notes: Sharing food with one's spouse by eating from the same plate as well eating from the same food is a *sunnah* of the Prophet ﷺ. This is something that unfortunately has become very rare in the modern society as everything now comes in its own portion. Also people are so conscious of hygiene and germs and so forth, but *Subhan-Allah,* the Messenger of Allah ﷺ is eating from the left over food of his wife who happens to be menstruating. If this does not help develop love between the spouse, then what will? While it is understandable to be weary of eating the leftover food of a stranger, there should be a distinction between a stranger and one's spouse with whom one is intimate.

الحديث الثاني و العشرون

حَدَّثَنَا الحَكَمُ بْنُ نَافِعٍ، قَالَ: أَخْبَرَنَا شُعَيْبٌ، عَنِ الزُّهْرِيِّ، قَالَ: حَدَّثَنِي عَامِرُ بْنُ سَعْدٍ، عَنْ سَعْدِ بْنِ أَبِي وَقَّاصٍ، أَنَّهُ أَخْبَرَهُ أَنَّ رَسُولَ اللَّهِ صَلَّى اللَّهُ عَلَيْهِ وَسَلَّمَ قَالَ

إِنَّكَ لَنْ تُنْفِقَ نَفَقَةً تَبْتَغِي بِهَا وَجْهَ اللَّهِ إِلَّا أُجِرْتَ عَلَيْهَا، حَتَّى مَا تَجْعَلُ فِي فَمِ امْرَأَتِكَ

~ Hadīth 22 ~

FEEDING ONE'S SPOUSE

Narrated Sa'd bin Abi Waqqas:
The Messenger of Allah ﷺ said, "You will be rewarded
for whatever you spend for Allah's sake, even the food
you place in your spouse's mouth."

Sahih al-Bukhari 56

Notes: In this modern world of busy schedules and social media,
families live in the same homes yet live isolated lives. There
is very little time where the husband and wife get to spend
together, yet the spouses can make use of these gentle gestures to
exhibit their love and affection. Feeding your spouse with your
own hands now and then can transform a normal dinner time
into moments of quality time for bonding and rekindling the
flames of love in the marriage.

Also these actions with the right intentions can become acts of
spiritual closeness to your Lord, as the Prophet ﷺ mentioned
that spending on and feeding one's family is a *sadaqa.*

إِذَا أَنْفَقَ الرَّجُلُ عَلَى أَهْلِهِ يَحْتَسِبُهَا فَهُوَ لَهُ صَدَقَةٌ

*"If a man spends on his family with the hope of reward from Allah, it
will be a sadaqa for him."* (Sahih al-Bukhari 55)

الحديث الثالث و العشرون

حَدَّثَنَا هِشَامُ بْنُ عَمَّارٍ قَالَ: حَدَّثَنَا إِسْمَاعِيلُ بْنُ عَيَّاشٍ، عَنْ بَجِيرِ بْنِ سَعْدٍ، عَنْ خَالِدِ بْنِ مَعْدَانَ، عَنِ الْمِقْدَامِ بْنِ مَعْدِيكَرِبَ الزُّبَيْدِيِّ، عَنْ رَسُولِ اللَّهِ صَلَّى اللَّهُ عَلَيْهِ وَسَلَّمَ، قَالَ: مَا كَسَبَ الرَّجُلُ كَسْبًا أَطْيَبَ مِنْ عَمَلِ يَدِهِ، وَمَا أَنْفَقَ الرَّجُلُ عَلَى نَفْسِهِ وَأَهْلِهِ وَوَلَدِهِ وَخَادِمِهِ، فَهُوَ صَدَقَةٌ

~ *Hadīth 23* ~

PROVIDING FOR ONE'S SPOUSE

Narrated by Miqdam bin Ma'dikarib:
The Messenger of Allah ﷺ said: "No man earns
anything better than that which he earns with his own
hands. And whatever a man spends on himself, his
wife, his child and his servant, that is *sadaqa*."

Sunan Ibn Majah 2138

Notes: Providing for one's family and spouse is such a worthy
action that one is rewarded not only in the hereafter as a means
of charity written in their book of deeds, but also one can see
the fruits and blessings in this life when done with sincerity.
Likewise this can be in other ways like looking after one's spouse
and family or cooking and feeding one's family, such that each of
the spouses can play their own role in serving the family. Know
that whatever wealth and effort one puts into their marriage and
family will not be in vain, rather they will be rewarded and also
Allah will compensate them in other ways such that the fruits
will be seen either immediately or in the future:

وَمَا أَنفَقْتُم مِّن شَيْءٍ فَهُوَ يُخْلِفُهُ وَهُوَ خَيْرُ الرَّازِقِينَ
*"Whatever thing you spend [in His cause] - He will compensate it; and
He is the best of providers."*
(Al-Qur'an s34 v39)

الحديث الرابع و العشرون

حَدَّثَنِي مَحْمُودُ بْنُ غَيْلَانَ، حَدَّثَنَا عَبْدُ الرَّزَّاقِ، أَخْبَرَنَا مَعْمَرٌ، عَنِ الزُّهْرِيِّ، عَنْ عَلِيِّ بْنِ حُسَيْنٍ، عَنْ صَفِيَّةَ بِنْتِ حُيَيٍّ، قَالَتْ: كَانَ رَسُولُ اللَّهِ صَلَّى اللَّهُ عَلَيْهِ وَسَلَّمَ مُعْتَكِفًا فَأَتَيْتُهُ أَزُورُهُ لَيْلًا، فَحَدَّثْتُهُ ثُمَّ قُمْتُ فَانْقَلَبْتُ، فَقَامَ مَعِي لِيَقْلِبَنِي، وَكَانَ مَسْكَنُهَا فِي دَارِ أُسَامَةَ بْنِ زَيْدٍ، فَمَرَّ رَجُلَانِ مِنَ الْأَنْصَارِ، فَلَمَّا رَأَيَا النَّبِيَّ صَلَّى اللَّهُ عَلَيْهِ وَسَلَّمَ أَسْرَعَا، فَقَالَ النَّبِيُّ صَلَّى اللَّهُ عَلَيْهِ وَسَلَّمَ: عَلَى رِسْلِكُمَا إِنَّهَا صَفِيَّةُ بِنْتُ حُيَيٍّ» فَقَالَا سُبْحَانَ اللَّهِ يَا رَسُولَ اللَّهِ قَالَ: إِنَّ الشَّيْطَانَ يَجْرِي مِنَ الْإِنْسَانِ مَجْرَى الدَّمِ، وَإِنِّي خَشِيتُ أَنْ يَقْذِفَ فِي قُلُوبِكُمَا سُوءًا، أَوْ قَالَ: شَيْئًا

~ *Hadīth 24* ~

WALKING SPOUSE HOME

Narrated Safiyyah bint Huyay:
"While the Messenger of Allah ﷺ was in *I`tikaf*, I
visited him at night, we spoke then I stood up to leave.
He came to accompany me to where I was staying,
(Usama bin Zaid's house). Two Ansari men passed by,
and seeing the Prophet ﷺ they hastened away. The
Prophet said. "Don't hurry! It is only Safiyyah, the
daughter of Huyay (i.e. my wife)." They said, "Subhan
Allah! O Allah's Messenger ﷺ! (How dare we suspect
you?)" He said, "Satan circulates in the human mind as
blood circulates in it, and I was afraid that Satan might
throw an evil thought or something into your hearts."

Sahih al-Bukhari 3281

Notes: This *hadith* is another beautiful example of where the
Prophet ﷺ went out of his way to spend some quality time
with his wife by walking her home. Gestures such as these help
to allow the bond of companionship to develop between the
spouses. Often spouses spend only the bare minimum time with
each other and each one is busy with their own task. While this
is productive for work, it does not help the marital bond and
they need one another's company to get to know each other
personally. It is only then that feelings can develop in their hearts.
One should also be careful of public displays of affection or
compromising situations which can be perceived the wrong way:

دَعْ مَا يَرِيبُكَ إِلَى مَا لاَ يَرِيبُكَ

"Leave what makes you in doubt for what does not make you in doubt"
(Jami' al-Tirmidhi 2518)

الحديث الخامس و العشرون

حَدَّثَنَا قُتَيْبَةُ، وَهَنَّادٌ، وَأَبُو كُرَيْبٍ، وَأَحْمَدُ بْنُ مَنِيعٍ، وَمَحْمُودُ بْنُ غَيْلَانَ، وَأَبُو عَمَّارٍ، قَالُوا: حَدَّثَنَا وَكِيعٌ، عَنِ الْأَعْمَشِ، عَنْ حَبِيبِ بْنِ أَبِي ثَابِتٍ، عَنْ عُرْوَةَ، عَنْ عَائِشَةَ

أَنَّ النَّبِيَّ صَلَّى اللَّهُ عَلَيْهِ وَسَلَّمَ قَبَّلَ بَعْضَ نِسَائِهِ، ثُمَّ خَرَجَ إِلَى الصَّلَاةِ وَلَمْ يَتَوَضَّأْ، قَالَ: قُلْتُ: مَنْ هِيَ إِلَّا أَنْتِ؟ فَضَحِكَتْ

~ *Hadīth 25* ~

KISSING ONE'S SPOUSE

Narrated by 'A'isha:
"The Messenger of Allah ﷺ kissed one of his wives
and then left for prayer without performing ablution."
Urwa (the narrator) says, "I asked 'Aisha, "It must
have been you?" 'Aisha smiled."

Sunan al-Tirmidhi 86

Notes: Kissing one's spouse is a *sunnah* of the Messenger of
Allah ﷺ. Kissing is an expression of love and affection which
helps to build the marital bond between the spouses. Based on
this *hadīth* it is recommended to kiss one's wife when one leaves
the home as well as greeting the wife with a kiss when one
enters the home. Kissing was such a common occurrence in the
Messenger's ﷺ day to day life that it has been reported that he
would even kiss his wives while fasting:

كَانَ يُقَبِّلُ وَهُوَ صَائِمٌ

"He would kiss while fasting" (Sahih Muslim 1106)

The messenger ﷺ had great control over himself thus not
violating the fast, but this is just an example of how regular these
expressions were. He ﷺ would even at times, kiss in a very
passionate way by sucking on his wife's tongue:

كَانَ يُقَبِّلُهَا وَيَمُصُّ لِسَانَهَا

"He would kiss her and suck her tongue" (Sunan Abi Dawud 2386)

الحديث السادس و العشرون

حَدَّثَنَا قَبِيصَةُ، حَدَّثَنَا سُفْيَانُ، عَنْ

مَنْصُورٍ، عَنْ أُمِّه

عَنْ عَائِشَةَ، قَالَتْ

كَانَ النَّبِيُّ صَلَّى اللهُ عَلَيْهِ وَسَلَّمَ يَقْرَأُ

الْقُرْآنَ وَرَأْسُهُ فِي حَجْرِي وَأَنَا حَائِضٌ

~ *Hadīth 26* ~

LYING ON SPOUSE'S LAP

Narrated by `Aisha:
The Prophet ﷺ used to recite the Qur'an with his
head on my lap while I was menstruating.

Sahih al-Bukhari 7549

Notes: Allah has made the spouses a source of comfort, love and
tranquillity for each other, Allah says:

وَمِنْ آيَاتِهِ أَنْ خَلَقَ لَكُمْ مِنْ أَنْفُسِكُمْ أَزْوَاجًا لِتَسْكُنُوا إِلَيْهَا وَجَعَلَ بَيْنَكُمْ مَوَدَّةً وَرَحْمَةً
*And of His signs is that He created for you from yourselves mates that
you may find tranquillity in them; and He placed between you affection
and mercy.* (Al-Quran s30 v21)

One should seek these blessings that Allah has bestowed from
their spouse as these are the few legitimate avenues for comfort
and tranquillity. One may not find the comfort straight away,
rather they need to be patient and allow their spouse to open
themselves up to them and learn to trust them. Once mutual trust
is built, it is only then one can hope to find the comfort and really
appreciate the favours Allah has bestowed, and see the fruits of
the blessings.

الحديث السابع و العشرون

حَدَّثَنَا قُتَيْبَةُ، حَدَّثَنَا لَيْثٌ، عَنِ ابْنِ شِهَابٍ، عَنْ عُرْوَةَ، وَعَمْرَةَ بِنْتِ عَبْدِ الرَّحْمَنِ، أَنَّ عَائِشَةَ رَضِيَ اللَّهُ عَنْهَا زَوْجَ النَّبِيِّ صَلَّى اللَّهُ عَلَيْهِ وَسَلَّمَ قَالَتْ: وَإِنْ كَانَ رَسُولُ اللَّهِ صَلَّى اللَّهُ عَلَيْهِ وَسَلَّمَ لَيُدْخِلُ عَلَيَّ رَأْسَهُ وَهُوَ فِي الْمَسْجِدِ، فَأُرَجِّلُهُ، وَكَانَ لَا يَدْخُلُ الْبَيْتَ إِلَّا لِحَاجَةٍ إِذَا كَانَ مُعْتَكِفًا

~ *Hadīth 27* ~

COMBING SPOUSE'S HAIR

Narrated by `Aisha:
The Messenger of Allah ﷺ used to let his head through while he was in the mosque and I would comb his hair. He would not enter the house while in the state of *I'tikaf* except for necessity.

Sahih al-Bukhari 2029

Notes: The spouses are encouraged to adorn themselves for each other, as marriage is a way in which one can beautify themselves and help beautify their spouse. Many times you will find that individuals pay more effort to adorning themselves and are eager to look nice in front of others like their friends and relatives. Yet these same people will make very little effort for their spouse. How can one expect love and affection to develop in this manner? The wives of the Prophet ﷺ would comb his hair, oil his hair and even wash his hair as mentioned in a *hadith*:

فَأَغْسِلُ رَأْسَهُ

"And I would wash his hair" (Sunan Abi-Dawud)

One should remember that Allah has not only made the spouses from themselves, but He also has made them such that they compliment and beautify each other.

هُنَّ لِبَاسٌ لَكُمْ وَأَنْتُمْ لِبَاسٌ لَهُنَّ

"They are a clothing (covering) for you and you too are a clothing for them." (Al-Qur'an s2 v187)

الحديث الثامن و العشرون

وَحَدَّثَنَا مُحَمَّدُ بْنُ الْمُثَنَّى، حَدَّثَنَا أَبُو
عَاصِمٍ، قَالَ: سَمِعْتُ ابْنَ عَوْنٍ، عَنْ
إِبْرَاهِيمَ، عَنِ الْأَسْوَدِ، قَالَ: انْطَلَقْتُ
أَنَا وَمَسْرُوقٌ، إِلَى عَائِشَةَ رَضِيَ اللَّهُ
عَنْهَا، فَقُلْنَا لَهَا: " أَكَانَ رَسُولُ اللَّهِ
صَلَّى اللَّهُ عَلَيْهِ وَسَلَّمَ يُبَاشِرُ وَهُوَ صَائِمٌ؟
قَالَتْ: نَعَمْ، وَلَكِنَّهُ كَانَ أَمْلَكَكُمْ لِإِرْبِهِ
أَوْ مِنْ أَمْلَكِكُمْ لِإِرْبِهِ

~ *Hadīth 28* ~

EMBRACING ONE'S SPOUSE

Narrated by Aswad:
I and Masruq went to 'A'isha and asked her if the
Messenger of Allah ﷺ embraced his wives while
fasting, she said: "Yes; but he had greater control over
his desire than you," or "he was one who had control
over his desire."

Sahih Muslim 1106

Notes: Embracing is a universal language of care, affection and
love. The Prophet ﷺ would regularly embrace his wives as can
be seen in this *hadith* and the numerous other *ahadith* on this
topic. Embracing one's spouse reminds them that you care for
them and are showing your affection towards them.
Another *hadith* mentions he ﷺ embraced his wives when they
were menstruating, and he ﷺ gave the guidance that one can still
show affection within the limits set by the *shariah*:

كَانَ رَسُولُ اللَّهِ صلى الله عليه وسلم يُبَاشِرُ نِسَاءَهُ فَوْقَ الإِزَارِ وَهُنَّ حُيَّضٌ

*The Messenger of Allah ﷺ contacted and embraced his wives over the
waist-wrapper when they were menstruating.* (Sahih Muslim 294)
Another *hadith* shows that one should embrace one's spouse
when they may be sad or upset. 'Aisha mentions:

الْتَفَتَ فَأَسْرَعْتُ الْمَشْىَ فَأَدْرَكَنِي فَاحْتَضَنَنِي

*"I turned away and walked quickly, but he caught up with me and
embraced me"* (Sunan Ibn Majah 1980)

الحديث التاسع و العشرون

حَدَّثَنَا أَبُو صَالِحٍ الْأَنْطَاكِيُّ مَحْبُوبُ بْنُ مُوسَى، أَخْبَرَنَا أَبُو إِسْحَاقَ يَعْنِي الْفَزَارِيَّ، عَنْ هِشَامِ بْنِ عُرْوَةَ، عَنْ أَبِيهِ، وَعَنْ أَبِي سَلَمَةَ عَنْ عَائِشَةَ، رَضِيَ اللَّهُ عَنْهَا، أَنَّهَا كَانَتْ مَعَ النَّبِيِّ صَلَّى اللَّهُ عَلَيْهِ وَسَلَّمَ فِي سَفَرٍ قَالَتْ: فَسَابَقْتُهُ فَسَبَقْتُهُ عَلَى رِجْلَيَّ، فَلَمَّا حَمَلْتُ اللَّحْمَ سَابَقْتُهُ فَسَبَقَنِي فَقَالَ: هَذِهِ بِتِلْكَ السَّبْقَةِ

~ *Hadīth 29* ~

RACING WITH ONE'S SPOUSE

Narrated by 'Aisha:
While she was on a journey with the Messenger of
Allah ﷺ she said, "I had a sprinting race with him
which I won. Later when I put on weight, I had another
race with him and this time he won. He said: This win
is for the previous race."

Sunan Abi Dawud 2578

Notes: Competing and having fun with one's spouse is an
important part of a healthy and fulfilling marital relationship.
Spending recreational time together allows the development of a
mutual bond and keeps the excitement of marriage kindled well
into the later part of your lives. In a normal marriage the husband
and wife can be two completely different people with different
ways of thinking, but these enjoyable, humorous and exciting
events can bring a spark which is otherwise hidden. One is also
encouraged to compete in good things, Allah says:

أُولَٰئِكَ يُسَارِعُونَ فِي الْخَيْرَاتِ وَهُمْ لَهَا سَابِقُونَ
*"It is those who hasten to good deeds, and they outstrip [others]
therein."* (Al-Quran s23 v61)

So the husband and wife can compete with each other in good
things, this is healthy competition which will bring them closer
to Allah and also bring them closer to each other as they start to
enjoy their mutual companionship.

الْحَدِيثُ الثَّلَاثُونَ

حَدَّثَنَا أَبُو بَكْرِ بْنُ أَبِي شَيْبَةَ قَالَ: حَدَّثَنَا يَزِيدُ بْنُ هَارُونَ قَالَ: أَنْبَأَنَا هِشَامٌ الدَّسْتُوَائِيُّ، عَنْ يَحْيَى بْنِ أَبِي كَثِيرٍ، عَنْ أَبِي سَلَّامٍ، عَنْ عَبْدِ اللَّهِ بْنِ الْأَزْرَقِ، عَنْ عُقْبَةَ بْنِ عَامِرٍ الْجُهَنِيِّ، عَنِ النَّبِيِّ صَلَّى اللهُ عَلَيْهِ وَسَلَّمَ قَالَ: إِنَّ اللَّهَ لَيُدْخِلُ بِالسَّهْمِ الْوَاحِدِ الثَّلَاثَةَ الْجَنَّةَ: صَانِعَهُ يَحْتَسِبُ فِي صَنْعَتِهِ الْخَيْرَ، وَالرَّامِيَ بِهِ، وَالْمُمِدَّ بِهِ وَقَالَ رَسُولُ اللَّهِ صَلَّى اللهُ عَلَيْهِ وَسَلَّمَ: «ارْمُوا وَارْكَبُوا، وَأَنْ تَرْمُوا أَحَبُّ إِلَيَّ مِنْ أَنْ تَرْكَبُوا، وَكُلُّ مَا يَلْهُو بِهِ الْمَرْءُ الْمُسْلِمُ بَاطِلٌ، إِلَّا رَمْيَهُ بِقَوْسِهِ، وَتَأْدِيبَهُ فَرَسَهُ، وَمُلَاعَبَتَهُ امْرَأَتَهُ، فَإِنَّهُنَّ مِنَ الْحَقِّ

سنن ابن ماجه ٢٨١١

~ *Hadīth 30* ~

PLAYING WITH ONE'S SPOUSE

Narrated by 'Uqbah bin 'Amir Al-Juhani:
The Prophet ﷺ said: "Allah will admit three people to Paradise by the virtue of an arrow: The one who makes it; seeking reward, the one who shoots it, and the one who hands it to him." And the Messenger of Allah ﷺ said: "Shoot and ride, for shooting is dearer to me than riding. All entertainment that a Muslim engages in is futile except for archery, training one's horse and playing with one's spouse, for these are from the truth."

Sunan Ibn Majah 2811

Notes: The Prophet ﷺ placed great significance in playing with one's spouse that can be seen in this *hadith* where he ﷺ says that genuine playful entertainment is limited to three; one being the playing with one's spouse. Playing with one's spouse will allow good quality bonding time in a happy and exciting environment where each can relax and allow themselves to open up with each other. There is plenty of opportunity to try and make time for 'playtime' between the spouses. One only has to be creative and you will find these moments become moments of joy, excitement and happiness and it can do wonders in developing care, compassion and affection in the relationship.

الحديث الحادي و الثلاثون

حَدَّثَنَا عَلِيٌّ، حَدَّثَنَا ابْنُ عُلَيَّةَ، عَنْ حُمَيْدٍ، عَنْ أَنَسٍ، قَالَ: كَانَ النَّبِيُّ صَلَّى اللهُ عَلَيْهِ وَسَلَّمَ عِنْدَ بَعْضِ نِسَائِهِ، فَأَرْسَلَتْ إِحْدَى أُمَّهَاتِ الْمُؤْمِنِينَ بِصَحْفَةٍ فِيهَا طَعَامٌ، فَضَرَبَتِ الَّتِي النَّبِيُّ صَلَّى اللهُ عَلَيْهِ وَسَلَّمَ فِي بَيْتِهَا يَدَ الْخَادِمِ، فَسَقَطَتِ الصَّحْفَةُ فَانْفَلَقَتْ، فَجَمَعَ النَّبِيُّ صَلَّى اللهُ عَلَيْهِ وَسَلَّمَ فِلَقَ الصَّحْفَةِ، ثُمَّ جَعَلَ يَجْمَعُ فِيهَا الطَّعَامَ الَّذِي كَانَ فِي الصَّحْفَةِ، وَيَقُولُ: غَارَتْ أُمُّكُمْ ثُمَّ حَبَسَ الْخَادِمَ حَتَّى أُتِيَ بِصَحْفَةٍ مِنْ عِنْدِ الَّتِي هُوَ فِي بَيْتِهَا، فَدَفَعَ الصَّحْفَةَ الصَّحِيحَةَ إِلَى الَّتِي كُسِرَتْ صَحْفَتُهَا، وَأَمْسَكَ الْمَكْسُورَةَ فِي بَيْتِ الَّتِي كُسِرَتْ

~ *Hadīth 31* ~

PATIENCE WITH SPOUSE'S ANGER

Narrated by Anas:
While the Prophet ﷺ was in one of his wife's houses, one of the mothers of the believers sent a meal in a dish. The wife at whose house the Prophet ﷺ was, struck the hand of the servant, causing the dish to fall and break. The Prophet ﷺ gathered the broken pieces of the dish and then started collecting the food which had been in the dish and said, "Your mother (my wife) felt jealous." Then he detained the servant till a dish was brought from the wife at whose house he was. He gave the intact dish to the wife whose dish had been broken and kept the broken one at the house where it had been broken.

Sahih al-Bukhari 5225

Notes: Any marriage is bound to have some instances where there is a dispute which might lead to anger. Even the Prophet ﷺ would have such in his household, but such anger should not be allowed to escalate. Another *hadith* shows where the Prophet ﷺ and his wife were actually arguing and 'Aisha's voice became louder than his and her father (Abu Bakr), when he witnessed this wanted to scold her, but the Prophet ﷺ came in the way to protect her; he ﷺ then said; "See how I saved you?":

فَحَالَ النَّبِيُّ صَلَّى اللهُ عَلَيْهِ وَسَلَّمَ، بَيْنَهُ وَبَيْنَهَا، قَالَ: فَلَمَّا خَرَجَ أَبُو بَكْرٍ جَعَلَ النَّبِيُّ صَلَّى اللهُ
عَلَيْهِ وَسَلَّمَ، يَقُولُ لَهَا يَتَرَضَّاهَا: أَلَا تَرَيْنَ أَنِّي قَدْ حُلْتُ بَيْنَ الرَّجُلِ وَبَيْنَكِ

"So the Prophet stood between them and when Abu Bakr left, he said to her, "See how I saved you from him?" (Musnad Ahmad 18394)

الحديث الثاني و الثلاثون

حَدَّثَنَا ابْنُ بَشَّارٍ، حَدَّثَنَا يَحْيَى، حَدَّثَنَا ابْنُ عَجْلَانَ، عَنِ الْقَعْقَاعِ، عَنْ أَبِي صَالِحٍ، عَنْ أَبِي هُرَيْرَةَ، قَالَ: قَالَ رَسُولُ اللَّهِ صَلَّى اللَّهُ عَلَيْهِ وَسَلَّمَ رَحِمَ اللَّهُ رَجُلًا قَامَ مِنَ اللَّيْلِ فَصَلَّى، وَأَيْقَظَ امْرَأَتَهُ، فَإِنْ أَبَتْ، نَضَحَ فِي وَجْهِهَا الْمَاءَ، رَحِمَ اللَّهُ امْرَأَةً قَامَتْ مِنَ اللَّيْلِ فَصَلَّتْ، وَأَيْقَظَتْ زَوْجَهَا، فَإِنْ أَبَى، نَضَحَتْ فِي وَجْهِهِ الْمَاءَ

~ *Hadīth 32* ~

AWAKING SPOUSE FOR PRAYER

Narrated by Abu Huraira:
The Messenger of Allah ﷺ said, "May Allah have
mercy on a man who gets up at night and prays, and
awakens his wife; if she refuses, he sprinkles water on
her face.
May Allah have mercy on a woman who gets up at
night and prays, and awakens her husband; if he
refuses, she sprinkles water on his face."

Sunan Abi Dawud 1308

Notes: Husband and wife helping each other in obedience to
their creator is a beautiful partnership that transcends the mere
materialistic realm. The Prophet ﷺ would spend long nights in
prayer, and near the end when it was time to offer *witr* he would
wake his wife so that she could also pray:

فَإِذَا أَرَادَ أَنْ يُوتِرَ أَيْقَظَنِي فَأَوْتَرْتُ

*"Whenever he intended to offer the witr prayer, he used to wake me up
and I would offer the witr prayer too."* (Sahih al-Bukhari 997)

The reward for encouraging someone to do good is such that the
one who guides will be rewarded the same as the one who did
the action:

مَنْ دَلَّ عَلَى خَيْرٍ, فَلَهُ مِثْلُ أَجْرِ فَاعِلِه

*"He who guides (others) to an act of goodness, will have a reward
similar to that of its doer."* (Sahih Muslim 173)

الحديث الثالث و الثلاثون

حَدَّثَنَا عَبْدُ الْغَفَّارِ بْنُ دَاوُدَ، حَدَّثَنَا
يَعْقُوبُ بْنُ عَبْدِ الرَّحْمَنِ، عَنْ عَمْرِو بْنِ
أَبِي عَمْرٍو، عَنْ أَنَسِ بْنِ مَالِكٍ رَضِيَ اللَّهُ
عَنْهُ، قَالَ: قَدِمَ النَّبِيُّ صَلَّى اللَّهُ عَلَيْهِ وَسَلَّمَ
خَيْبَرَ، فَلَمَّا فَتَحَ اللَّهُ عَلَيْهِ الْحِصْنَ ذُكِرَ لَهُ
جَمَالُ صَفِيَّةَ بِنْتِ حُيَيِّ بْنِ أَخْطَبَ، وَقَدْ
قُتِلَ زَوْجُهَا، وَكَانَتْ عَرُوسًا، فَاصْطَفَاهَا
رَسُولُ اللَّهِ صَلَّى اللَّهُ عَلَيْهِ وَسَلَّمَ لِنَفْسِهِ،
فَخَرَجَ بِهَا حَتَّى بَلَغْنَا سَدَّ الرَّوْحَاءِ حَلَّتْ
فَبَنَى بِهَا، ثُمَّ صَنَعَ حَيْسًا فِي نِطَعٍ صَغِيرٍ
ثُمَّ قَالَ رَسُولُ اللَّهِ صَلَّى اللَّهُ عَلَيْهِ وَسَلَّمَ:
آذِنْ مَنْ حَوْلَكَ ، فَكَانَتْ تِلْكَ وَلِيمَةَ
رَسُولِ اللَّهِ صَلَّى اللَّهُ عَلَيْهِ وَسَلَّمَ عَلَى صَفِيَّةَ،
ثُمَّ خَرَجْنَا إِلَى الْمَدِينَةِ قَالَ: فَرَأَيْتُ رَسُولَ
اللَّهِ صَلَّى اللَّهُ عَلَيْهِ وَسَلَّمَ يُحَوِّي لَهَا وَرَاءَهُ
بِعَبَاءَةٍ، ثُمَّ يَجْلِسُ عِنْدَ بَعِيرِهِ، فَيَضَعُ رُكْبَتَهُ
فَتَضَعُ صَفِيَّةُ رِجْلَهَا عَلَى رُكْبَتِهِ حَتَّى تَرْكَبَ

~ Hadīth 32 ~

HELPING SPOUSE ONTO VEHICLE

Narrated Anas bin Malik:
The Prophet ﷺ came to Khaibar, Allah made him
victorious and he conquered the town by breaking
the enemy's defence. The beauty of Safiyyah bint
Huyay bin Akhtab was mentioned to him and that her
husband had been killed while she was a new bride.
Allah's Messenger ﷺ selected her for himself and he
set out in her company till he reached *Sadd-ar-Rawha'*
where her menses was over and he married her. Then a
meat dish was prepared and served on a small leather
sheet. Allah's Messenger ﷺ then said to me, "Invite
those who are around you." So that was the *walima*
given by Allah's Messenger ﷺ for Safiyyah. After
that we proceeded to Madina and I saw that Allah's
Messenger ﷺ was covering her with a cloak while
she was behind him. Then he kneeled and let Safiyyah
place her foot on his knees to climb onto her camel.

Sahih al-Bukhari 2235

Notes: The Prophet ﷺ was newly married and he helped his wife
onto her ride by allowing her to step on his knees! This is the
care, respect and humility the Prophet ﷺ expressed towards his
wives, we can act upon this *sunnah* in a much easier way which
can be as simple as opening the car door for our spouses.

الحديث الرابع و الثلاثون

حَدَّثَنَا هَنَّادٌ قَالَ: حَدَّثَنَا مُلَازِمُ بْنُ عَمْرٍو، قَالَ: حَدَّثَنِي عَبْدُ اللَّهِ بْنُ بَدْرٍ، عَنْ قَيْسِ بْنِ طَلْقٍ، عَنْ أَبِيهِ طَلْقِ بْنِ عَلِيٍّ قَالَ: قَالَ رَسُولُ اللَّهِ صَلَّى اللَّهُ عَلَيْهِ وَسَلَّمَ: إِذَا الرَّجُلُ دَعَا زَوْجَتَهُ لِحَاجَتِهِ فَلْتَأْتِهِ، وَإِنْ كَانَتْ عَلَى التَّنُّورِ

~ Hadīth 34 ~

FULFILLING SPOUSE'S NEED

Narrated by Talq bin Ali
The Messenger of Allah ﷺ said, "When a man calls his
wife to fulfil his needs, then let her come, even if she is
at the oven (cooking)."

Jami` at-Tirmidhi 1160

Notes: Fulfilling the physical or even the emotional needs of the
spouse is a vital part of marriage. Allah knows us all well and He
understands the nature of human beings and has therefore made
the spouses a means of comfort and tranquillity for each other.
One should not treat it as a burden, rather it is a means of reward
and is a pillar of building a marital bond, intimacy and affection.
The Prophet ﷺ said that fulfilling the needs of one's spouse is
Sadaqa, thus rewarded;

وَفِي بُضْعِ أَحَدِكُمْ صَدَقَةٌ، قَالُوا: يَا رَسُولَ الله، أَيَأْتِي أَحَدُنَا شَهْوَتَهُ وَيَكُونُ لَهُ فِيهَا أَجْرٌ؟ قَالَ:
أَرَأَيْتُمْ لَوْ وَضَعَهَا فِي حَرَامٍ أَكَانَ عَلَيْهِ فِيهَا وِزْرٌ؟ فَكَذَلِكَ إِذَا وَضَعَهَا فِي الْحَلَالِ كَانَ لَهُ أَجْرٌ

"And in marital relations there is a Sadaqa. The companions asked: O
Messenger of Allah, is there reward for satisfying one's desires? He
ﷺ *said: Tell me, if one fulfils these unlawfully, would it not be a sin?*
Similarly, if one fulfils these lawfully, he should have a reward."
(Sahih Muslim 1006)

الحديث الخامس و الثلاثون

حَدَّثَنَا عَبْدُ اللَّهِ بْنُ مَسْلَمَةَ، أَخْبَرَنَا أَفْلَحُ بْنُ حُمَيْدٍ، عَنِ الْقَاسِمِ، عَنْ عَائِشَةَ، قَالَتْ: كُنْتُ أَغْتَسِلُ أَنَا وَالنَّبِيُّ صَلَّى اللهُ عَلَيْهِ وَسَلَّمَ مِنْ إِنَاءٍ وَاحِدٍ، تَخْتَلِفُ أَيْدِينَا فِيه

~ Hadīth 35 ~

TAKING A BATH WITH ONE'S SPOUSE

Narrated by 'Aisha:
"The Prophet ﷺ and I used to take a bath together
from a single pot of water, and our hands used to go
into the pot after each other in turn."

Sahih al-Bukhari 261

Notes: There are various avenues one can find to spend quality
time with one's spouse, and to make these moments exciting
and memorable. The Prophet ﷺ would have a bath with his
wife, together sharing the same water bucket, to the extent they
would enjoy and have fun together and tease each other. Another
hadith mentions that they would compete with each other to
use the water from the one bucket due to the scarcity of water,
such that they would plead to each other to leave some water for
themselves:

كُنْتُ أَغْتَسِلُ أَنَا وَرَسُولُ اللهِ صَلَّى اللهُ عَلَيْهِ وَسَلَّمَ مِنْ إِنَاءٍ وَاحِدٍ، يُبَادِرُنِي وَأُبَادِرُهُ. حَتَّى يَقُولَ
دَعِي لِي . وَأَقُولُ أَنَا: دَعْ لِي
*"I used to perform ghusl with the Messenger of Allah ﷺ from one
vessel. He would compete with me and I would with him for the water,
until he would say: 'Leave some for me' and I would say: 'Leave some
for me.'"* (Sunan al-Nasa'i 240)

الحديث السادس و الثلاثون

حَدَّثَنَا مُحَمَّدُ بْنُ يَحْيَى قَالَ: حَدَّثَنَا
سَعِيدُ بْنُ سُلَيْمَانَ قَالَ: حَدَّثَنَا مُحَمَّدُ
بْنُ مُسْلِمٍ قَالَ: حَدَّثَنَا إِبْرَاهِيمُ بْنُ
مَيْسَرَةَ، عَنْ طَاوُسٍ، عَنِ ابْنِ عَبَّاسٍ،
قَالَ: قَالَ رَسُولُ اللَّهِ صَلَّى اللَّهُ
عَلَيْهِ وَسَلَّمَ
لَمْ نَرَ لِلْمُتَحَابَّيْنِ مِثْلُ النِّكَاحِ

~ *Hadīth 36* ~

LOVING ONE'S SPOUSE

Narrated by Ibn Abbas:
The Messenger of Allah ﷺ said: "There is nothing like
marriage for two people to love one another."

Sunan Ibn Majah 1847

Notes: Allah has made marriage the legitimate avenue for
two separate people to find love, compassion, selflessness,
companionship and intimacy in each other. Unfortunately, the
world around us has painted a glossy picture of love which
is based on lust, desire and self satisfaction. This can cause
confusion within the spouses, as often one's marital expectations
are based on the worldly perception. You should remember that
your union is ordained by Allah and He has placed blessings in
the marriage. We just need to see it in an Islamic perspective and
put our contribution towards this union.
The Prophet ﷺ has advised that a good way to build love is to
express one another's feelings and to say nice, kind and loving
words to each other. Express your love to each other as the
Prophet ﷺ said;

إِذَا أَحَبَّ أَحَدُكُمْ أَخَاهُ فَلْيُعْلِمْهُ إِيَّاهُ
"When one of you loves another then they should express it to them."
(Jami` at-Tirmidhi 2392)

الحديث السابع و الثلاثون

حَدَّثَنَا أَبُو بَكْرِ بْنُ أَبِي شَيْبَةَ قَالَ: حَدَّثَنَا وَكِيعٌ، عَنْ هِشَامِ بْنِ عُرْوَةَ، عَنْ أَبِيهِ، عَنْ عَائِشَةَ، قَالَتْ: مَا ضَرَبَ رَسُولُ اللَّهِ صَلَّى اللَّهُ عَلَيْهِ وَسَلَّمَ خَادِمًا لَهُ، وَلَا امْرَأَةً، وَلَا ضَرَبَ بِيَدِهِ شَيْئًا

~ *Hadīth 37* ~

NOT TO ABUSE ONE'S SPOUSE

Narrated by 'Aisha:
"The Messenger of Allah ﷺ never struck a servant of
his, nor a woman, nor stuck anyone with his hands."

Sunan Ibn Majah 1984

Notes: Every relationship should be based on respect, tolerance
and mutual understanding. This is especially the case in a marital
relationship where two people will be in each other's presence
day and night. In the process there will surely be instances
of annoyance but this should never lead to anger that breeds
violance. The Prophet ﷺ who was the guide and the role model
for the whole of humanity did not strike a woman nor a child nor
anyone.

قَالَ فَخَدَمْتُهُ فِي السَّفَرِ وَالْحَضَرِ، مَا قَالَ لِي لِشَىْءٍ صَنَعْتُهُ لِمَ صَنَعْتَ هَذَا هَكَذَا وَلاَ لِشَىْءٍ لَمْ
أَصْنَعْهُ لِمَ لَمْ تَصْنَعْ هَذَا هَكَذَا

*Anas said," So, I served him at home and on journeys. If I did anything,
he never asked me why I did it, and if I refrained from doing anything,
he never asked me why I refrained from doing it. (Sahih Bukhari 2678)*
The Prophet ﷺ questioned the logic of how one can beat their
spouse yet later carry on as if nothing has happend;

بِمَ يَضْرِبُ أَحَدُكُمُ امْرَأَتَهُ ضَرْبَ الْفَحْلِ، أَوِ العَبْدِ، ثُمَّ لَعَلَّهُ يُعَانِقُهَ
*"How can you beat your wife like an animal then sleep with them
later?" (Sahih al-Bukhari 6042)*

الحديث الثامن و الثلاثون

حَدَّثَنَا أَبُو بَكْرِ بْنُ أَبِي شَيْبَةَ، حَدَّثَنَا مَرْوَانُ بْنُ مُعَاوِيَةَ، عَنْ عُمَرَ بْنِ حَمْزَةَ الْعُمَرِيِّ، حَدَّثَنَا عَبْدُ الرَّحْمَنِ بْنُ سَعْدٍ، قَالَ: سَمِعْتُ أَبَا سَعِيدٍ الْخُدْرِيَّ، يَقُولُ: قَالَ رَسُولُ اللهِ صَلَّى اللهُ عَلَيْهِ وَسَلَّمَ: إِنَّ مِنْ أَشَرِّ النَّاسِ عِنْدَ اللهِ مَنْزِلَةً يَوْمَ الْقِيَامَةِ، الرَّجُلَ يُفْضِي إِلَى امْرَأَتِهِ، وَتُفْضِي إِلَيْهِ، ثُمَّ يَنْشُرُ سِرَّهَا

~ Hadīth 38 ~

NOT TO DISCLOSE SECRETS OF ONE'S SPOUSE

Narrated by Abu Sa'id al-Khudri:
The Messenger of Allah ﷺ said, "The worst of people in the sight of Allah on the Day of judgment is the man who goes to his wife and she comes to him, and then he divulges her secret".

Sahih Muslim 1437

Notes: In order for any relationship to be successful, there has to be a sense of trust between the parties, this is especially the case in marriage. Two, otherwise completely separate and different people suddenly are in wedlock so they need to be able to express themselves and share private and intimate details with each other. To disclose such details to others is a breach and betrayal of trust and hinders progress in the relationship. This is of great importance in this age of social media where everyone's private life is open and exposed to the world and strangers get to know of intimate and private information as well as see pictures. One should be conscious and careful of exposing oneself and family to the evil eye, as its true:
The Prophet ﷺ said that the evil eye can have an effect;

الْعَيْنُ حَقٌّ

"The effect of evil eye is true." (Sahih al-Bukhari 5740)
Also the Prophet ﷺ said that being jealous and protective for one's family and womenfolk is from *Iman*.

إِنَّ الْغَيْرَةَ مِنَ الْإِيمَانِ

"Protective jealousy is from Iman" (Shu'b al-Iman of Baihaqi 10308)

الحديث التاسع و الثلاثون

حَدَّثَنَا مُحَمَّدُ بْنُ مُقَاتِلٍ، أَخْبَرَنَا عَبْدُ اللَّهِ، أَخْبَرَنَا الأَوْزَاعِيُّ، قَالَ: حَدَّثَنِي يَحْيَى بْنُ أَبِي كَثِيرٍ، قَالَ: حَدَّثَنِي أَبُو سَلَمَةَ بْنُ عَبْدِ الرَّحْمَنِ، قَالَ: حَدَّثَنِي عَبْدُ اللَّهِ بْنُ عَمْرِو بْنِ العَاصِ، قَالَ: قَالَ رَسُولُ اللَّهِ صَلَّى اللَّهُ عَلَيْهِ وَسَلَّمَ: يَا عَبْدَ اللَّهِ، أَلَمْ أُخْبَرْ أَنَّكَ تَصُومُ النَّهَارَ وَتَقُومُ اللَّيْلَ؟ قُلْتُ: بَلَى يَا رَسُولَ اللَّهِ، قَالَ: فَلَا تَفْعَلْ، صُمْ وَأَفْطِرْ، وَقُمْ وَنَمْ، فَإِنَّ لِجَسَدِكَ عَلَيْكَ حَقًّا، وَإِنَّ لِعَيْنِكَ عَلَيْكَ حَقًّا، وَإِنَّ لِزَوْجِكَ عَلَيْكَ حَقًّا

~ *Hadith 39* ~

SPOUSE'S RIGHT

Narrated by `Abdullah bin `Amr bin Al-`As:
The Messenger of Allah ﷺ said, "O `Abdullah! Have
I not been informed that you fast all day and stand in
prayer all night?" I said, "Yes, O Allah's Messenger!"
He said, "Do not do that! Observe fast some days, and
do not fast some days, stand for prayer at night and
also sleep at night. Your body has a right over you,
your eyes have a right over you and your spouse has a
right over you."

Sahih al-Bukhari 5199

Notes: Islam is such a religion that it explains all things and
places everything into perspective. While it is a worthy deed for
someone to want to fast or to stand all night in prayer, however,
as these acts of worship to Allah will infringe on the rights of
the spouse, Allah is then not in need of such worship that harms
another being. One needs to understand that there is a balance
and that balance will create harmony, not only in the marriage
but also in one's lives. The Prophet ﷺ mentions that any
violation of the rights of one's spouse or anyone else will have to
be answered on the day of judgement:

لَتُؤَدُّنَّ الْحُقُوقَ إِلَى أَهْلِهَا يَوْمَ الْقِيَامَةِ حَتَّى يُقَادَ لِلشَّاةِ الْجَلْحَاءِ مِنَ الشَّاةِ الْقَرْنَاءِ
*"Rights will be given their due on the day of judgement, such that the
hornless sheep would get its claim from the horned sheep."*
(Sahih Muslim 2582)

Therefore, one should be very careful of the spouse's rights, even
if they don't ask for it.

الحديث الأربعون

حَدَّثَنَا عَبْدُ اللَّهِ بْنُ يُوسُفَ، حَدَّثَنَا اللَّيْثُ، قَالَ: حَدَّثَنِي ابْنُ الهَادِ، عَنْ عَبْدِ الرَّحْمَنِ بْنِ القَاسِمِ، عَنْ أَبِيهِ، عَنْ عَائِشَةَ، قَالَتْ: مَاتَ النَّبِيُّ صَلَّى اللَّهُ عَلَيْهِ وَسَلَّمَ وَإِنَّهُ لَبَيْنَ حَاقِنَتِي وَذَاقِنَتِي، فَلَا أَكْرَهُ شِدَّةَ المَوْتِ لِأَحَدٍ أَبَدًا، بَعْدَ النَّبِيِّ صَلَّى اللَّهُ عَلَيْهِ وَسَلَّمَ

~ *Hadīth 40* ~

DYING IN SPOUSE'S ARMS

Narrated by `Aisha:
"The Prophet ﷺ died while he was between my chest and chin, so I never dislike the death agony for anyone after the Prophet ﷺ."

Sahih al-Bukhari 4446

Notes: The husband and wife should endeavour to live their lives with each other such that their marital bond gets stronger and stronger with every day that goes by. It may be hard at first to get used to a person with perhaps a different way of thinking, but this can be done with effort and perseverance. If the spouses have lived a life of obedience to Allah, then they can hope that their spouse and offspring will continue to make *dua* for them and be a means of ongoing reward. The Prophet ﷺ said;

إِذَا مَاتَ الإِنْسَانُ انْقَطَعَ عَنْهُ عَمَلُهُ إِلاَّ مِنْ ثَلاَثَةٍ إِلاَّ مِنْ صَدَقَةٍ جَارِيَةٍ أَوْ عِلْمٍ يُنْتَفَعُ بِهِ أَوْ وَلَدٍ صَالِحٍ يَدْعُو لَهُ

"When a person dies, their deeds come to an end, except for three; recurring charity, or knowledge (by which people) benefit, or a pious child, who prays for them." (Sahih Muslim 1631)

The end of one's life will be according to the life they have lived. We should realise and make changes now, as it is the last actions that counts towards or final deeds. The Prophet ﷺ said;

وَإِنَّمَا الأَعْمَالُ بِخَوَاتِيمِهَا

"Surely the results of deeds are based on a person's last actions"
(Sahih al-Bukhari 6463)